Quilts
from
Aunt Amy

❧❧ Mary Tendall Etherington ❧❧
and Connie Tesene

Martingale
& COMPANY

BOTHELL, WASHINGTON

CREDITS

President . . . . Nancy J. Martin
CEO/Publisher . . . . Daniel J. Martin
Associate Publisher . . . . .Jane Hamada
Editorial Director . . . . Mary V. Green
Design and Production Manager . . . . Cheryl Stevenson
Technical Editor . . . . Ursula Reikes
Copy Editor . . . . Tina Cook
Illustrator . . . . Laurel Strand
Photographer . . . . Brent Kane
Cover Designer . . . . Stan Green
Text Designer . . . . Trina Stahl
Proofreader . . . . Leslie Phillips

Quilts from Aunt Amy
© 1999 by Mary Tendall Etherington and Connie Tesene
Martingale & Company
PO Box 118
Bothell, WA 98041-0118 USA
www.patchwork.com

Printed in Hong Kong
04 03 02 01 00 99   6 5 4 3

MISSION STATEMENT

We are dedicated to providing quality products
and service by working together to
inspire creativity and to enrich the lives we touch.

That Patchwork Place is an imprint of Martingale & Company.

Library of Congress Cataloging-in-Publication Data

Etherington, Mary Tendall,
Quilts from Aunt Amy / Mary Tendall Etherington &
Connie Tesene.
        p.   cm.
ISBN 1-56477-258-6
1. Patchwork—Patterns.   2. Quilting—Patterns.
I. Tesene, Connie .   II. Title.
TT835.E87   1999
746.46'041—dc21   99-10296
                                                              CIP

DEDICATION

TO THE MEMORY of Amy Anderson who, while living, never got any praise, credit, or appreciation for her many talents and hard work.

ACKNOWLEDGMENTS

OUR THANKS TO:

Norma Sommerdorf, whose mother was Amy's sister. She graciously helped collect Amy's belongings, her crocheted tablecloth, the Peter and Polly book, the woodburnt box, the spinning wheel brought to the United States from Sweden, and the assorted linens and patterns from Amy's collection. We got a terrific sense of Amy's personality from her various handicrafts.

Mary's mother, Hazel Larson, for her fond memories of Aunt Amy.

Mary's aunt, Mildred Anderson, for passing along the sampler quilt.

Contents

Introduction

AMY WAS MY great aunt on my mother's side, which means she was an old woman when I was just a teenager. Looking back on her hobbies and pastimes is like looking at myself in the mirror. Because she is my only ancestor who enjoyed quiltmaking—as well as rugmaking, woodburning, crocheting, and sewing, not to mention making scrapbooks, watching birds, and reading—I feel a real connection with Amy. I wish she were alive today because we would have so much in common.

My mom tells stories about how her brothers and sisters loved visiting Amy's house. They liked to snoop through her things, try on her fancy hats, read her many books, and eat her wonderful doughnuts. My mother, Hazel Larson, remembers:

When I was young, my Aunt Amy lived on a farm a half mile from where we lived. She kept house for her two brothers who were not married. In those days, the mail carrier did not go to every farm, but there were several mailboxes at the corner of our grove. One of us had to take the mail to Amy, Charlie, and Albert. I liked to do it because Amy always had good cookies and donuts as well as a bookcase full of favorite books, like Black Soil *and* Prairie Rose. *She made a picture book called* Peter and Polly *that was also a favorite. She had a baby doll and a suitcase of clothes that she made for the doll. And what fun it was to swing in the hammock that hung between two trees in her front yard.*

A SAMPLER QUILT dated 1898 was passed on to me by my mom's sister, Mildred Anderson. I didn't know of its existence until I received it, so I can only guess at its origin. In 1898 Amy would have been twenty-one years old and already an accomplished needlewoman. My guess is that she set the collection of blocks together at that time. Some blocks are beautifully pieced, while others are haphazardly sewn, suggesting that she had learned to piece different blocks over the years and in 1898 got around to sewing them together. It had to have been tied at a later date, since the blue yarn she used is acrylic. The binding is stitched by machine and the quilt is in very good condition. I can only guess at its complete story.

At Country Threads, we had been thinking about what to do with Aunt Amy's sampler quilt for a long time. To do something in 1998 seemed especially appropriate because the quilt was made in 1898. When we approached Martingale & Company with the idea, they suggested that we make quilts based on some of the blocks in Amy's sampler. This was a challenge for us, since many of the blocks they selected were ones that we were not familiar with and would probably never have considered making. But the result is nothing short of spectacular, even if we do say so ourselves.

MARY TENDALL ETHERINGTON

Bernhardina "Amy" Anderson
1877–1964

IT HAS BEEN my privilege to work on this book with Mary. Since I don't have a relative, living or deceased, who made quilts, it's been fun to borrow Amy for a while and imagine that she is part of my own family. It's also been a wonderful experience to see the personal memorabilia the Anderson family collected for this book. It renews my desire to make quilts for my children, grandchildren, friends, and family so that I will be remembered in the same special way.

CONNIE TESENE

❧ AMY'S CRAFTS ❧
By Norma Sommerdorf

AMY WAS *a needlewoman. With her busy hands she left a lasting legacy of pillowcases and sheets with crocheted hems. There are towels with tatted hems, crocheted and tatted doilies, and a large crocheted tablecloth almost too precious to use.*

Heavy wool quilts made from men's suits, filled with sheep's wool from the farm, were left on the beds upstairs. There are thick wool socks she knitted from yarn spun on her mother's spinning wheel brought from Sweden in 1881.

She made numerous aprons, embroidered across the front with fancy stitches, as gifts for her sisters and nieces. She also tried her hand at other crafts, including woodburning.

And, there are quilts of many kinds, some sewn by machine for practicality, and some made entirely by hand for show.

AMY'S HATS
By Norma Sommerdorf

IN HER youth, Amy learned to make hats of all kinds. She is wearing a hat in almost every existing picture of her.

Amy went to Minneapolis to study millinery. A photograph taken around that time shows Amy at the Minnesota State Fair. Amy is seated on an automobile, wearing a beautiful hat. Behind the auto is her brother Henry and friends Paul, Tony, and Marie. Standing to the side of the automobile is a cardboard cutout of President Harding. The photo is dated 1909.

She made more practical hats in her later years, and hats for gardening were her trademark.

AMY'S NAME

AMY'S NAME wasn't Amy at all. It was Bernhardina. She had been born in Sweden, and she told of a voyage in the hold of a ship, with a trunk and other belongings marking her family's spot from that of the other passengers. She remembered being told to keep an eye on her brothers, Alec (six) and Henry (two), because her Mother was seasick much of the time.

After they arrived in New York they took the train to Iowa, where her mother had brothers and sisters who had come from Sweden earlier. They lived in Britt, Iowa, near the railroad track and the other Swedish relatives who preceded them. Her father got a job working on the railroad, which he kept until he had saved enough money to buy a farm in Orthel township.

When school started the teacher said that Bernhardina was too long and too hard a name for her to remember. "I'll call you Amy," she said. That name stuck and was her American name the rest of her life.

The Sampler Quilt

THE DIAGRAM BELOW corresponds to the blocks in Aunt Amy's sampler quilt, shown on the facing page. Several of the blocks are known by multiple names; the most common ones are listed here.

Flying X	Big Dipper Hourglass	Arabic Lattice	Four Crowns Union Star	Shoo Fly Eight-cornered Box	Variable Star Texas Star
Spider Web Boston Pavement	Double T Four T Square	Dove in the Window	Aunt Sukey's Choice	Odd Fellows Wild Goose Chase	Unknown
Formal Garden	Wedding Ring	Friendship Stars and Crosses	Grandmother's Fan Fan Patchwork	Drunkard's Path World's Path	Wonder of the World
Bow Tie	Live Oak Tree	Rolling Star Eight-Pointed Star	Mississippi Pink Meadow Lily	Flying Star Doves	Shooting Star Clay's Choice
Whirligig Design	Spinning Wheel	Bull's Eye	Album Katie's Choice	Rolling Pinwheel Whirligig Pinwheel	Goose Tracks
Mollie's Design	Tin Man	Joseph's Necktie	Noonday Lily North Carolina Lily	Double Z	Flower Basket Flower Pot
Slashed Album Flying Bats	Broken Dishes	Jacob's Ladder	Premium Star	Unknown	Robbing Peter to Pay Paul
Star of the East Silver and Gold	Spool Fred's Spool	Old Maid's Puzzle Double Triangle	Double T Four T Square	Variable Star Texas Star	Pullman's Puzzle

Country Threads Guidelines

ABOUT THE GUIDELINES

We've put together a few tips to get you started. If you need help with general techniques, refer to "Quiltmaking Basics" on pages 88–95 for detailed instructions.

FABRIC

◆ Use a variety of fabrics in many different shades and tints of a single color. Don't worry about cutting plaids and checks on-grain. Skewed patterns add to the old-time appearance of a quilt.

◆ Most yardage requirements call for an assortment of fabrics. When you see the amount given as "½ yd. *total* assorted fabrics," it means a combination of scraps, ⅛- yard pieces, fat quarters, and leftovers from other projects that total ½ yard.

◆ Don't worry about running out of a particular fabric. If you do run out, just substitute another fabric in its place. Using replacement fabrics will give your quilt a scrappy charm.

OVERDYEING

When a fabric we want to use seems too bright, we often resort to overdyeing it with tan dye. Overdyeing adds a warm, mellow look to almost any fabric. Restrict your overdyeing efforts to yardage—never dye a finished quilt; otherwise, the lights you used won't sparkle.

To overdye, place three yards of like-colored fabric in your washing machine. Set the water level to the lowest setting and double the amount of dye called for in the manufacturer's directions. Doubling the dye ensures a dark look, especially on dark-colored fabric. Reduce the amount of dye if you prefer a lighter shade. We use Rit tan dye, which can be found in grocery stores.

CONNECTOR SQUARES

♦ We like to use Mary Ellen Hopkins's "connector squares" method to add triangle corners to background squares. Place the connector square on the background piece in the appropriate corner. Stitch diagonally from corner to corner as shown in the piecing diagram for the block you are making. Trim the outside corner of the connector square.

Connector square

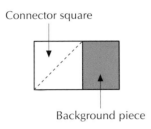

Background piece

Do not trim the corner of the background piece. Press the triangle toward the corner.

Trim outer corner
of connector square only.

CUTTING

♦ Cut a square once diagonally when you see this symbol: ⃞

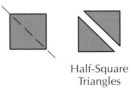

Half-Square
Triangles

♦ Cut a square twice diagonally when you see this symbol: ⊠

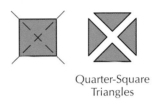

Quarter-Square
Triangles

♦ Cut borders across the width of the fabric and piece as necessary to achieve the required length. Add the top and bottom borders first, then add the side borders. Press the seam allowances toward the borders.

Star of the East Table Runner

EACH STAR OF the East block in our table runner contains thirty-two pieces, which is why this project has only three blocks. We used the same block to make a larger quilt, shown on page 18, but used only twelve pieces on a block background. If you prefer, you can refer to the instructions for that quilt to make twelve-piece blocks for the table runner.

Finished Table Runner: 17" x 44"

Finished Block: 9"

MATERIALS
42"-wide fabric

- ½ yd. cream print for block background
- 1 yd. red print for blocks, triangle units, border, and binding
- ¼ yd. red-and-tan check for triangle units
- 1⅓ yds. for backing
- ¼ yd. for binding

BLOCKS

From the cream print, cut:

- 4 strips, each 1¾" x 40", for strip unit

From the red print, cut:

- 4 strips, each 1¾" x 40", for strip unit
- 6 squares, each 3⅞" x 3⅞"; cut each square once diagonally to make 12 half-square triangles for triangle sections

From the red-and-tan check, cut:

- 12 squares, each 3⅞" x 3⅞"; cut each square once diagonally to make 24 half-square triangles for triangle sections

1. Make plastic or cardboard templates of templates 1 and 2 (page 17). Be sure to draw the center line on each template, and mark the positions of the light and dark fabrics.

2. Sew a 1¾"-wide cream strip to a 1¾"-wide red strip. Make 4 strip units.

3. Cut pieces as indicated in the following chart. You will have enough pieces to make 3 blocks.

Piece	Fabric	No. of Pieces	Dimensions
#1	Strip unit	12	Template 1*
#2	Strip unit	12	Template 2*
#3	Cream	12	2⅞" x 2⅞" ◨
#4	Cream	6	3⅜" x 3⅜" ◨
#5	Red	6	3⅜" x 3⅜" ◩

* Place the center line of the template on the seam line of the strip unit.

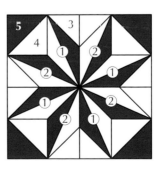

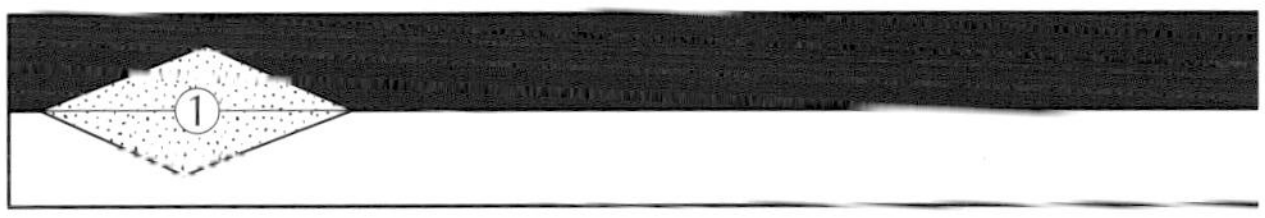

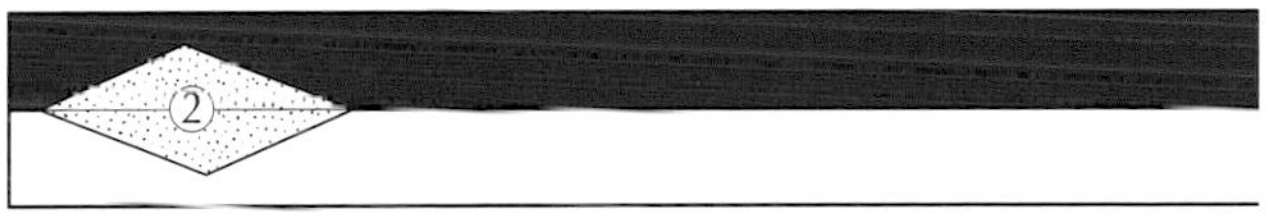

4. Join units to make one-quarter of a block. Be sure to use a piece #1 and a piece #2 for each quarter.

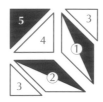

5. Join 4 quarters to complete the block.

6. Sew 3⅞" red and red-and-tan check triangles together to make half-square triangle units. Sew these and the remaining triangles together to make the side triangle sections.

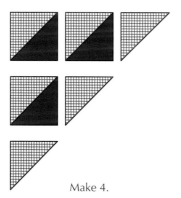

Make 4.

ASSEMBLY AND FINISHING

1. Arrange and sew the blocks and triangle sections in diagonal rows.

2. From the red print, cut 3 border strips, each 2½" x 40". Sew the borders to the quilt top, mitering the corners at opposite ends of the table runner. To sew the odd-angled seams at the sides, fold the table runner to align the edges of the binding as shown. Place the edge of a ruler along the folded edge of the table runner and draw a line on the binding along the edge of the ruler. Stitch on the line.

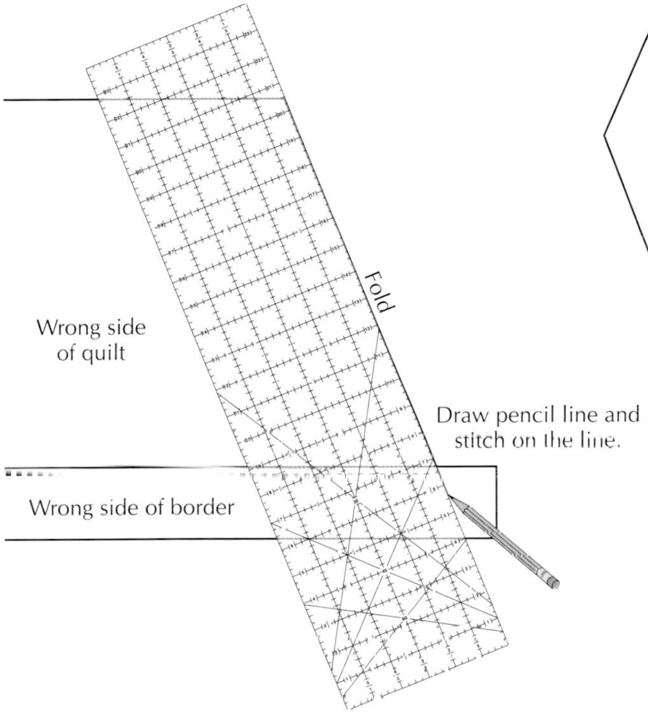

Wrong side of quilt

Fold

Draw pencil line and stitch on the line.

Wrong side of border

3. Layer the table runner with batting and backing; baste. Quilt as desired and bind the edges.

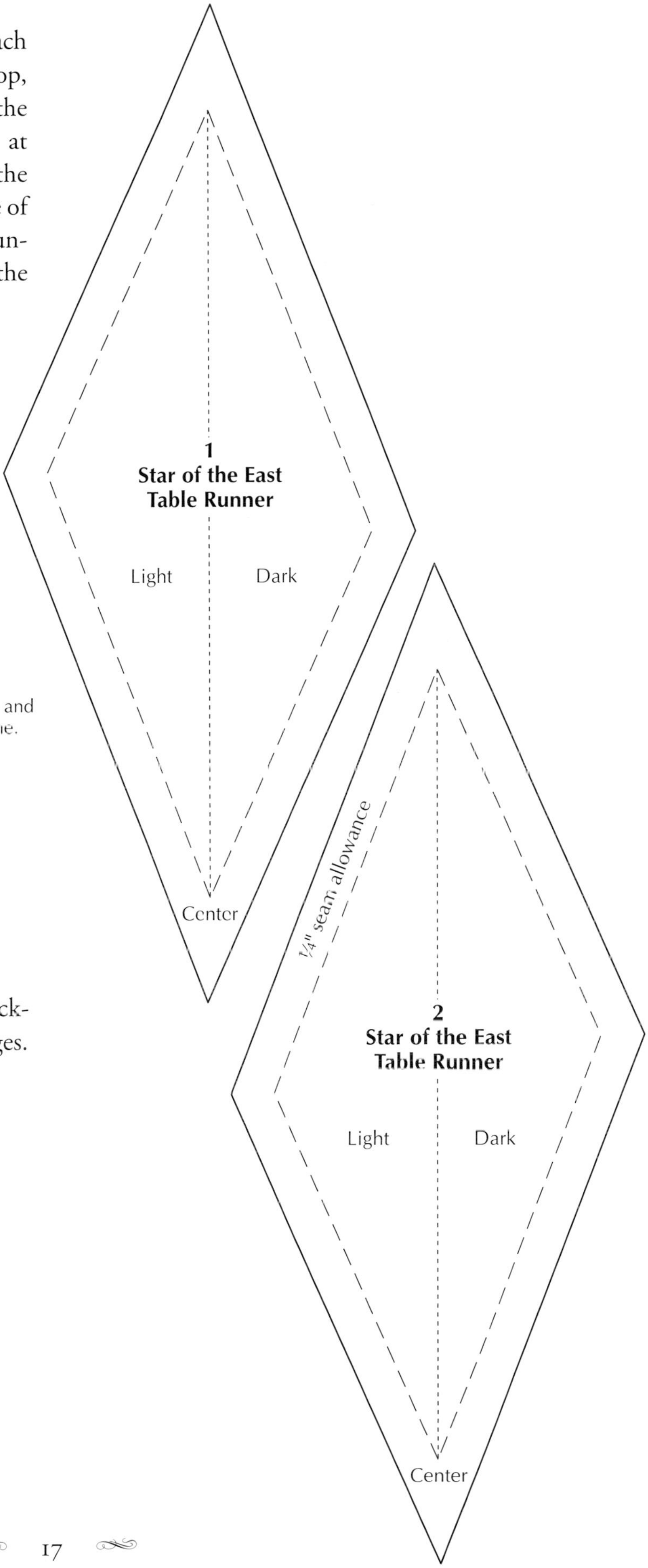

**1
Star of the East
Table Runner**

Light   Dark

¼" seam allowance

Center

**2
Star of the East
Table Runner**

Light   Dark

Center

Star of the East II

TO SIMPLIFY construction, we used fusible appliqué to make the Star of the East block. From a distance, the lack of seams is barely discernible.

Finished Quilt: 40" x 58"

Finished Block: 9"

MATERIALS
42"-wide fabric

- ◆ 1 fat quarter *each* of 15 tan prints for block backgrounds and pieced border
- ◆ ⅛ yd. *each* of 7 red prints for blocks and pieced border
- ◆ ⅛ yd. *each* of 8 blue prints for blocks and pieced border
- ◆ ¾ yd. blue print for outer border
- ◆ 2½ yds. for backing
- ◆ ⅓ yd. for binding
- ◆ Paper-backed fusible web

BLOCKS

Cut pieces as indicated in the following chart. You will have enough pieces to make 1 block. Make 7 red blocks and 8 blue blocks. Use the same blue or red fabric for individual blocks. Fuse pieces #3 and #4 to the 9½" square.

Piece	Fabric	No. of Pieces	Dimensions
#1	Tan	1	9½" x 9½"
#2	Blue or red	4	3" x 3" C
#3	Blue or red	4	Template 3
#4	Blue or red	4	Template 4

C *Connector squares (page 13).*

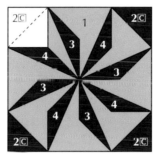 

Make 8 blue   Make 7 red

PIECED BORDER

From the tan fat quarters, cut:
- ◆ 16 rectangles, each 3" x 9½"
- ◆ 2 squares, each 3⅜" x 3⅜" cut each square once diagonally

From the red prints, cut:
- ◆ 20 squares, each 3" x 3" C

From the blue prints, cut:
- ◆ 12 squares, each 3" x 3" C
- ◆ 2 squares, each 3⅜" x 3⅜"; cut each square once diagonally

1. Sew a 3" blue connector square to each end of 6 tan rectangles. Repeat with red connector squares on the remaining rectangles.

Make 6 blue.

Make 10 red.

2. Sew the 3⅜" blue and tan triangles together to make corner squares.

Make 4.

ASSEMBLY AND FINISHING

1. Referring to the illustration at right, arrange and sew the blocks in 5 rows of 3 blocks each, alternating blue and red blocks.

2. Sew together 3 red and 2 blue rectangle units to make each side border. Sew the borders to the sides of the quilt top.

Make 2 for side borders.

3. Sew together 1 blue and 2 red rectangle units each to make the top and bottom borders. Add a blue/tan corner square to each end of the borders. Sew the borders to the top and bottom of the quilt top.

Make 2 for top and bottom borders.

4. From the blue print, cut 5 border strips, each 4½" x 40". Joining strips as needed to make borders of the correct length, sew the borders to the top and bottom of the quilt top, then to the sides.

5. Layer the quilt top with batting and backing; baste. Quilt as desired and bind the edges.

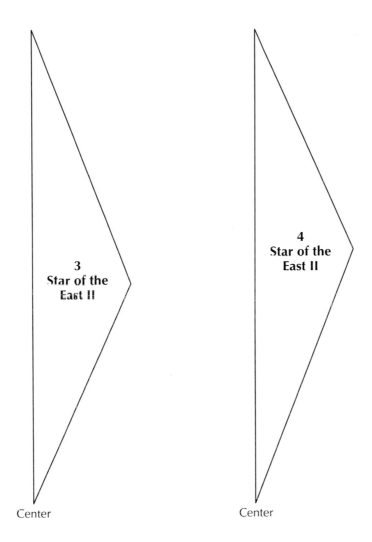

3
Star of the
East II

Center

4
Star of the
East II

Center

Mollie's Choice

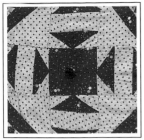

THE FUN PART of making blocks from Aunt Amy's quilt was experimenting, arranging, rearranging, and finally putting together the pieces to see what new pattern might occur. For Mollie's Choice, we cleaned up Amy's block to create a center medallion.

Finished Quilt: 50" x 50"
Finished Block: 11¼" x 11¼"

MATERIALS
42"-wide fabric

- ¼ yd. *each* of 4 tan prints for block backgrounds
- ¾ yd. *total* assorted blue and green prints for blocks and flying geese units
- ⅝ yd. blue check for background #1
- ½ yd. green print for background #2 and flying geese units
- 1¼ yds. floral print for flying geese units and outer border
- Scraps of red prints for blocks
- Scraps of orange and brown prints for blocks
- 3¼ yds. for backing
- ¼ yd. for binding

BLOCKS

Cut pieces as indicated in the following chart. The letter *r* after a number indicates that those pieces should be reversed. You will have enough pieces to make 1 block. Make 4 blocks.

Piece	Fabric	No. of Pieces	Dimensions
#1	Tan	3	4¼" x 4¼"
#1	Blue or green	1	4¼" x 4¼"
#2	Tan	4	1¾" x 4¼"
#3	Blue or green	8	Template 3
#4	Tan	8 and 8r	Template 4
#5	Tan	1	Template 5
#6	Red	1	Template 6
#7	Tan	1	1⅞" x 1⅞" ◻
#8	Orange	1	1½" x 1½"

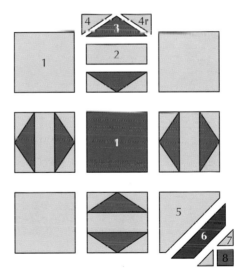

ASSEMBLY AND FINISHING

1. Referring to the photo on page 22, sew 4 blocks together to make the center section.

2. Make 4 corner units.

From the blue check, cut:
- 4 rectangles, each 4¼" x 15½"
- 4 rectangles, each 4¼" x 8"

From the green print, cut:
- 2 squares, each 6¼" x 6¼"; cut each square once diagonally to make 4 half-square triangles
- 4 squares, each 6⅝" x 6⅝"; cut each square twice diagonally to make 16 half-square triangles

Sew the blue check and green print pieces together, then add them to the sides of the center section.

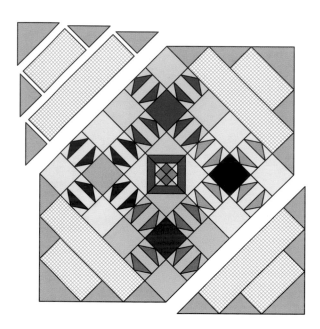

3. Cut pieces as indicated in the following chart. You will have enough pieces to make 64 flying geese units.

Piece	Fabric	No. of Pieces	Dimensions	
#1	Blue or green	16	5¼" x 5¼"	⊠
#2	Blue check	32	2⅞" x 2⅞"	◹
#3	Green print	32	2⅞" x 2⅞"	◹

Make 64.

4. Join 16 flying geese units to make each of 4 inner borders. Orient the geese so that they will point in the same direction all around the quilt.

5. Cut 2 squares, each 4⅞" x 4⅞", from the green print. Repeat with the floral print. Cut each square once diagonally. Sew the green and floral triangles together to make corner squares.

Make 4.

6. Sew pieced borders to opposite sides of the quilt top. Add a corner square to the remaining pieced borders and add these to the remaining sides.

7. From the floral print, cut 5 strips, each 5½" x 40". Joining strips as needed to make borders of the correct length, sew the outer border to the top and bottom of the quilt top, then to the sides.

8. Layer the quilt top with batting and backing; baste. Quilt as desired and bind the edges.

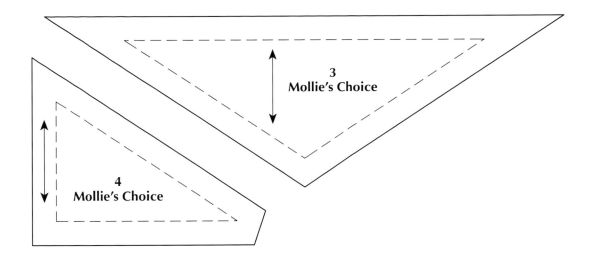

3
Mollie's Choice

4
Mollie's Choice

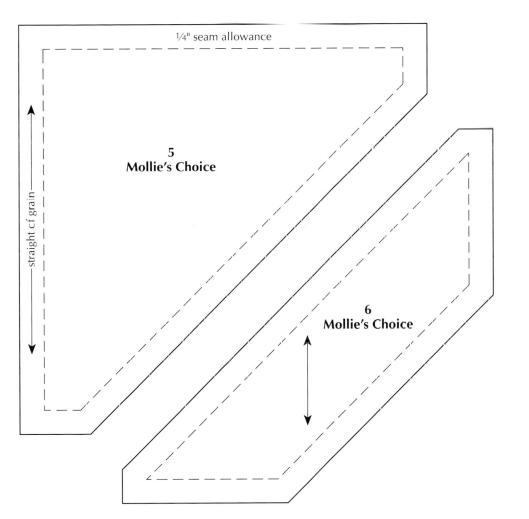

¼" seam allowance

straight cf grain

5
Mollie's Choice

6
Mollie's Choice

AUNT AMY'S Pullman Puzzle block looked like a flower to us. We liked the block, but we hesitated to sew the curved seams. Our solution was to cut the block into quarters, using connector squares in two corners and appliquéing a curved piece in the other corners to make the flower petal. We appliquéd the center to complete the block.

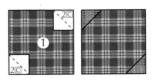

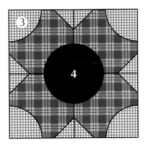

Finished Quilt: 40" x 40"

Finished Blocks: 8" x 8"

2. Cut pieces as indicated in the following chart. You will have enough pieces to make 4 blocks. Appliqué pieces #3 and #4.

Piece	Fabric	No. of Pieces	Dimensions
#1	Dark blue	16	4½" x 4½"
#2	Tan check	32	1¾" x 1¾" C
#3	Tan check	16	Template 3
#4	Gold check	4	Template 4

C *Connector squares (page 13).*

MATERIALS
42"-wide fabric

- ¾ yd. dark plaid for sunflowers
- 1¼ yds. tan check for block backgrounds
- ¼ yd. black solid for sunflower centers
- ⅞ yd. dark blue print for sunflowers and tulips
- ¼ yd. gold check for sunflower centers and tulips
- ¼ yd. white print for bowl
- ⅛ yd. medium blue print for bowl
- 1¼ yds. for backing
- ¼ yd. for binding

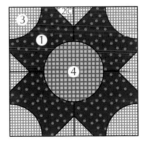

SUNFLOWER BLOCKS

1. Cut pieces as indicated in the following chart. You will have enough pieces to make 9 blocks. Appliqué pieces #3 and #4.

Piece	Fabric	No. of Pieces	Dimensions
#1	Dark plaid	36	4½" x 4½"
#2	Tan check	72	1¾" x 1¾" C
#3	Tan check	36	Template 3
#4	Black solid	9	Template 4

C *Connector squares (page 13).*

TULIP BLOCKS

Cut pieces as indicated in the following chart. The letter *r* after a number indicates that those pieces should be reversed. You will have enough pieces to make 6 blocks.

Piece	Fabric	No. of Pieces	Dimensions
#1	Dark blue	6 and 6r	Template 1
#2	Dark blue	6	2½" x 2½"
#3	Gold check	6	2½" x 2½"
#4	Tan check	3	3¼" x 3¼" ⊠
#5	Tan check	6 and 6r	Template 5
#6	Tan check	3	8⅞" x 8⅞" ◺

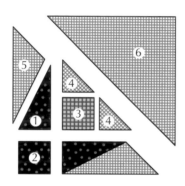

BOWL

Using pieces #1–6, cut and piece 1 bowl.

Piece	Fabric	No. of Pieces	Dimensions
#1	White print	1	2" x 24½"
#2	White print	2	1" x 24½"
#3	White print	1	3½" x 24½"
#4	Medium blue	2	1" x 24½"
#5	Medium blue	1	2" x 24½"
#6	Tan check	2	8½" x 8½" Ⓒ

Ⓒ *Connector squares (page 13).*

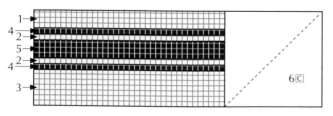

ASSEMBLY AND FINISHING

1. To make the center section, join 2 Tulip blocks, 1 Sunflower block, and the bowl. From the tan check, cut 2 strips, each 4½" x 24½". Sew these to the top and bottom of the center section.

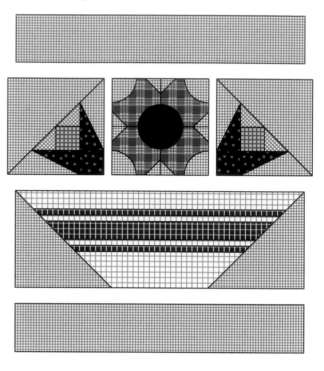

2. Arrange and sew the remaining Sunflower and Tulip blocks around the center section.

3. Layer the quilt top with batting and backing; baste. Quilt as desired and bind the edges.

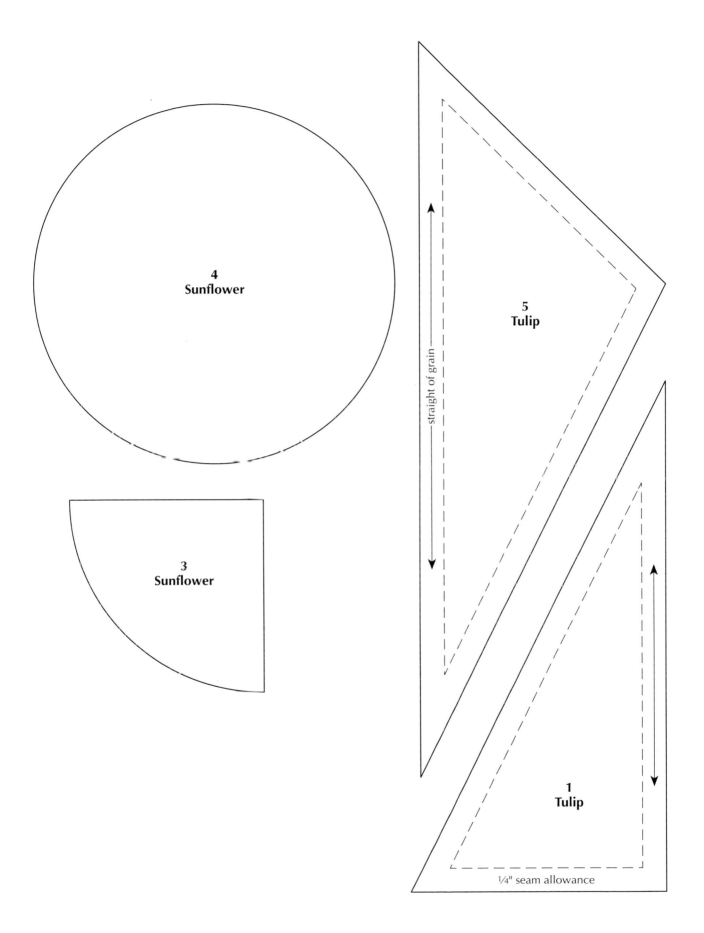

4
Sunflower

3
Sunflower

5
Tulip

straight of grain

1
Tulip

¼" seam allowance

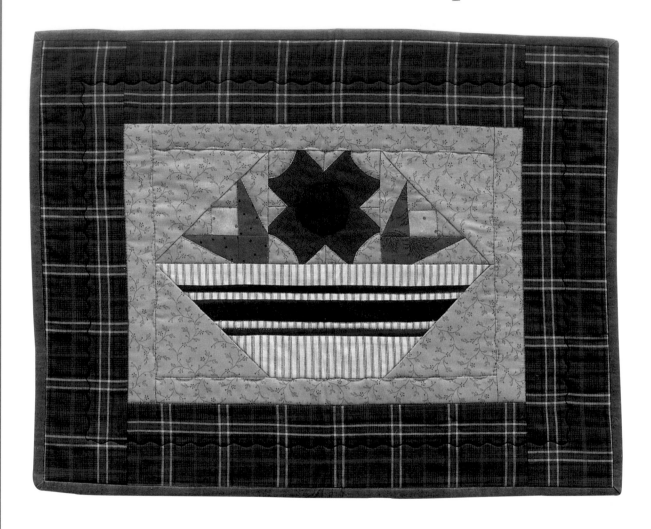

WE LIKED THE center portion of the quilt on page 26 so much we decided to reduce the design and make a quilt for a smaller space.

Finished Quilt: 20" x 16"

Finished Blocks: 4" x 4"

MATERIALS
42"-wide fabric

- ◆ Red, pink, orange, yellow, and brown scraps for sunflowers and tulips
- ◆ ³⁄₈ yd. light green print for background and inner border
- ◆ ⅛ yd. white print for bowl
- ◆ ⅛ yd. dark green print for bowl
- ◆ ¼ yd. green-and-red plaid for outer border
- ◆ ½ yd. for backing
- ◆ ⅛ yd. for binding

SUNFLOWER BLOCK

Cut pieces as indicated in the following chart. You will have enough pieces to make 1 block. Appliqué pieces #3 and #4.

Piece	Fabric	No. of Pieces	Dimensions
#1	Red	4	2½" x 2½"
#2	Light green	8	1¼" x 1¼" C
#3	Light green	4	Template 3
#4	Brown	1	Template 4

C *Connector squares (page 13).*

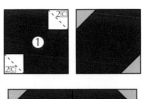

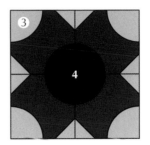

TULIP BLOCKS

Cut pieces as indicated in the following chart. You will have enough pieces to make 2 blocks.

Piece	Fabric	No. of Pieces	Dimensions
#1	Pink or orange	2 and 2r	Template 1
#2	Pink or orange	2	1½" x 1½"
#3	Yellow	2	1½" x 1½"
#4	Light green	1	2⅝" x 2⅝" ⊠
#5	Light green	2 and 2r	Template 5
#6	Light green	1	4⅞" x 4⅞" ◨

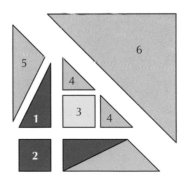

BOWL

Cut pieces as indicated in the following chart. You will have enough pieces to make 1 bowl.

Piece	Fabric	No. of Pieces	Dimensions
#1	White print	1	1¼" x 12½"
#2	White print	2	¾" x 12½"
#3	White print	1	2" x 12½"
#4	Dark green	2	¾" x 12½
#5	Dark green	1	1¼" x 12½"
#6	Light green	2	4½" x 4½" C
C	*Connector squares (page 13).*		

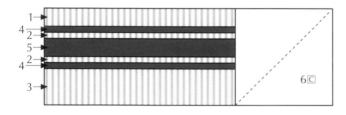

ASSEMBLY AND FINISHING

1. To make the center section, join 2 Tulip blocks, 1 Sunflower block, and the bowl.

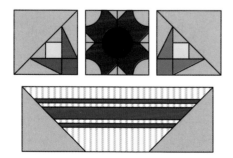

2. From the background fabric, cut 2 strips, each 1½" x 12½", for the top and bottom edges, and 2 strips, each 1½" x 10½", for the sides. Sew the border strips to the top and bottom first, then to the sides.

3. From the blue-and-red plaid, cut 2 strips, each 3½" x 14½", for the top and bottom edges, and 2 strips, each 3½" x 16½", for the sides. Sew the border strips to the top and bottom first, then to the sides.

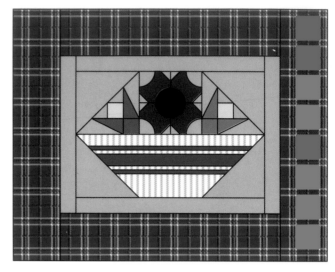

4. Layer the quilt top with batting and backing; baste. Quilt as desired and bind the edges.

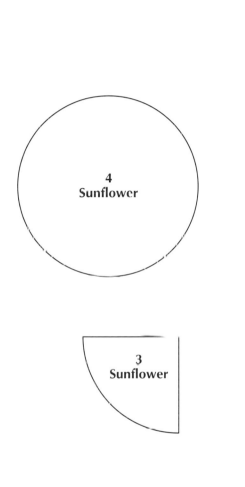

**4
Sunflower**

**3
Sunflower**

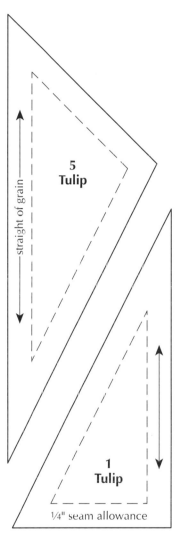

straight of grain

**5
Tulip**

**1
Tulip**

¼" seam allowance

Double Z

WHAT FUN TO play with fabric and just sew like crazy. We set our blocks in diagonal rows of like colors and used leftover light and dark centers for the border.

We think Aunt Amy was a woman ahead of her time. To make her Double Z block fit her quilt, she added spacer strips to two ends. We did too. Right on, Amy!

Finished Quilt: 47⅛" x 85⅜"

Finished Block: 9" x 9"

MATERIALS
42"-wide fabric

+ 2 yds. *total* assorted light prints for blocks
+ ½ yd. *total* assorted dark prints #1 for blocks
+ 2½ yds. *total* assorted dark prints #2 for blocks
+ 1 yd. light brown plaid for corner and side triangles
+ ⅜ yd. red print for inner border
+ ½ yd. dark brown plaid for outer border
+ 5 yds. for backing
+ ⅜ yd. for binding

BLOCKS

Using pieces #1–9, cut and piece 28 blocks. The cutting directions are for 1 block.

Piece	Fabric	No. of Pieces	Dimensions
#1	Dark #1	1	4¼" x 4¼" ⊠ *
#2	Light	1	4¼" x 4¼" ⊠ *
#3	Light	2	2" x 3½"
#4	Light	2	2⅜" x 2⅜" ◻
#5	Light	1	5¾" x 5¾" ⊠
#6	Dark #2	1	4¼" x 4¼" ⊠ *
#7	Dark #2	1	5¾" x 5¾" ⊠ **
#8	Dark #2	2	3⅛" x 3⅛" ◻
#9	Dark #2	2	1¼" x 9½"

* Use only 2 triangles for the block. Reserve the remainder for the pieced border.

** Use only 2 triangles for the block.

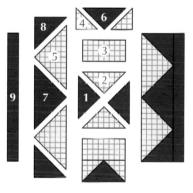

ASSEMBLY AND FINISHING

1. From the light brown plaid, cut 4 squares, each 14½" x 14½". Cut each square twice diagonally to make 16 side triangles (you will use only 14). Cut 2 squares, each 8¼" x 8¼". Cut each square once diagonally to make 4 corner triangles.

2. Arrange and sew the blocks and side triangles in diagonal rows. Add the corner triangles last.

3. Trim the triangles ¾" from the block corners.

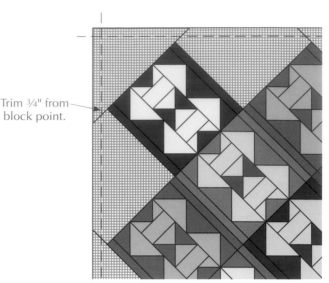

Trim ¾" from block point.

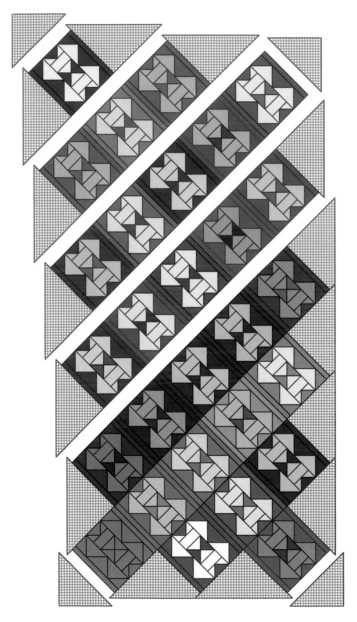

4. From the red print, cut 6 strips, each 1¼" x 40". Joining strips as needed to make borders of the correct length, sew the inner border to the top and bottom of the quilt top, then to the sides.

5. To make units for the pieced outer border, sew the remaining 4¼" light and dark triangles into squares.

Make 42.

6. From the dark brown plaid, cut 3 strips, each 3½" x 40", and 2 squares, each 3½" x 3½".

7. Arrange the triangle units and 3½" squares around the perimeter of the quilt top. Join the units. Add dark brown plaid strips to the joined units, trimming and seaming strips as necessary to reach the desired border lengths. Sew the border strips to the quilt top.

8. Layer the quilt top with batting and backing; baste. Quilt as desired and bind the edges.

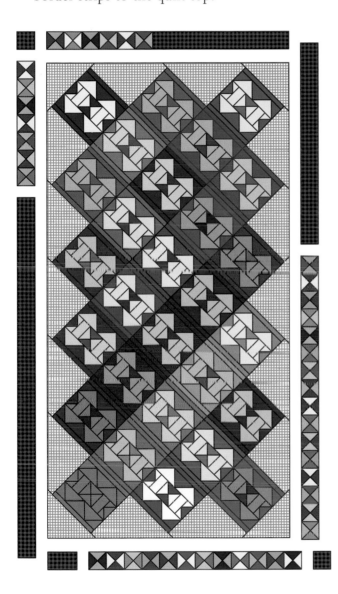

Flying Bats

BECAUSE WE ALWAYS make more than we need, we had enough Double Z blocks for two quilts. In this quilt, we surrounded the blocks with sashing strips made of triangle squares.

Finished Quilt: 36½" x 47"

Finished Blocks: 9" x 9"

MATERIALS
42"-wide fabric

- ◆ 1½ yds. *total* assorted light prints for blocks and pieced sashing
- ◆ ¼ yd. *total* assorted dark prints #1 for blocks
- ◆ 1¾ yds. *total* assorted dark prints #2 for blocks and pieced sashing
- ◆ ¼ yd. dark blue print for outer border
- ◆ 1½ yds. for backing
- ◆ ⅜ yd. for binding

BLOCKS

Cut pieces as indicated in the following chart. You will have enough pieces to make 1 block. Make 12 blocks.

Piece	Fabric	No. of Pieces	Dimensions	
#1	Dark #1	1	4¼" x 4¼"	⊠ *
#2	Light	1	4¼" x 4¼"	⊠ *
#3	Light	2	2" x 3½"	
#4	Light	2	2⅜" x 2⅜"	◻
#5	Light	1	5¾" x 5¾"	⊠
#6	Dark #2	1	4¼" x 4¼"	⊠ *
#7	Dark #2	1	5¾" x 5¾"	⊠ **
#8	Dark #2	2	3⅛" x 3⅛"	◻
#9	Dark #2	2	1¼" x 9½"	

* Use only 2 triangles for the block. Reserve the remainder for the pieced border.

** Use only 2 triangles for the block.

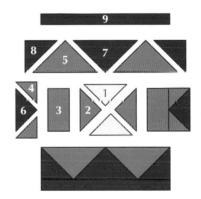

ASSEMBLY AND FINISHING

1. For the pieced sashing, cut 103 squares, each 2⅜" x 2⅜", from assorted light prints, and 103 squares, each 2⅜" x 2⅜", from assorted dark prints. Cut each square in half once diagonally to make a total of 206 light triangles and 206 dark triangles.

2. Join the light and dark triangles to make 206 triangle units.

Make 206.

3. Join 6 units to make each of 16 vertical sashing strips.

Make 16.

4. Sew 3 blocks and 4 sashing strips into horizontal rows, starting and ending each row with a sashing strip.

5. Make 5 horizontal sashing strips, joining 22 units for each. Join the rows of blocks and horizontal sashing strips.

6. From the dark blue print, cut 5 strips, each 2¼" x 40". Joining strips as necessary, sew the border to the top, bottom, and sides of the quilt.

7. Layer the quilt top with batting and backing; baste. Quilt as desired and bind the edges.

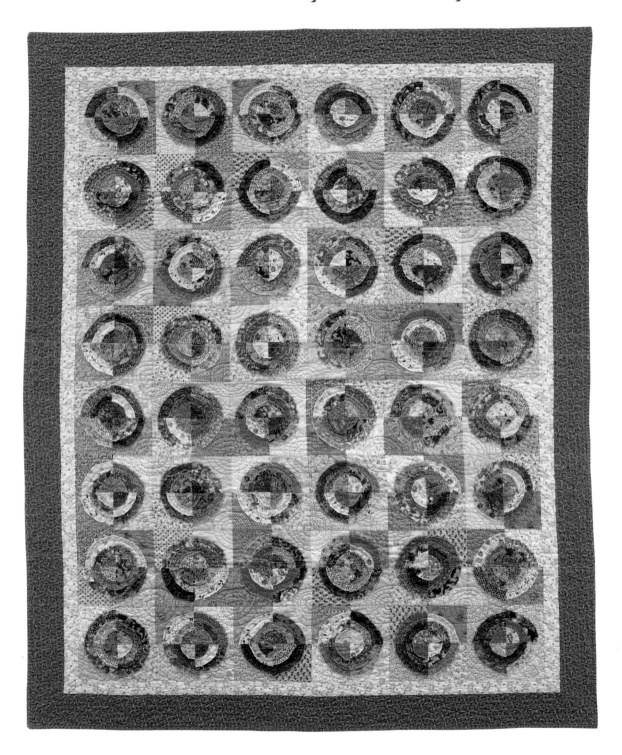

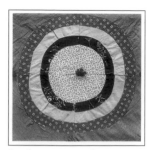

OUR RELUCTANCE TO piece curved seams gave birth to the raw-edged Bull's-Eye block. This is the most relaxing quilt we've ever made! We cut the circles freehand, and nothing had to match except the corners of the squares. Machine washing the quilt after it was quilted added texture. Since the circles and fabrics don't need to match, this quilt would make a perfect group project.

We've had more positive feedback about 21st-Century Bull's-Eye than about any other quilt we've ever done. "It looks like you just pulled it out of the trunk in grandma's attic," our friend Cheryl Barkema told us, while Mary Baker said, "It's great to have something new and different—a new technique with a new result! I love it!"

Finished Quilt: 58" x 74"

Finished Block: 8" x 8"

MATERIALS
42"-wide fabric

+ 3¼ yds. *total* assorted tan prints for backgrounds (or 48 squares, each 9" x 9")
+ 2½ yds. *total* assorted prints for large circles (or 48 squares, each 8" x 8")
+ 1½ yds. *total* assorted prints for medium circles (or 48 squares, each 6" x 6")
+ ¾ yd. *total* assorted prints for small circles (or 48 squares, each 4" x 4")
+ ½ yd. yellow print for inner border
+ 1 yd. blue print for outer border
+ 3⅝ yds. for backing
+ ⅜ yd. for binding

BULL'S-EYE BLOCK

Cut pieces as indicated in the following chart. You will have enough pieces to make 48 blocks.

Piece	Fabric	No. of Pieces	Dimensions
#1	Tan	48	9" x 9"
#2	Prints	48	8" x 8"
#3	Prints	48	6" x 6"
#4	Prints	48	4" x 4"

1. Fold each of the 8", 6", and 4" squares in quarters and cut a quarter-circle freehand.

2. Center a large circle on a 9" background square. Stitch around the circle, ¼" from the raw edge. Turn the block over and trim the background fabric inside the circle.

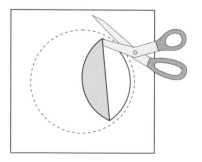

3. Center a medium circle on top of the large circle. Stitch around the medium circle, ¼" from the raw edge. Turn the block over and trim the large circle within the stitching.

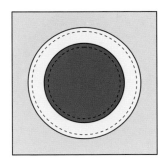

4. Center a small circle on top of the medium circle. Stitch around the small circle, ¼" from the raw edge. Turn the block over and trim the medium circle within the stitching.

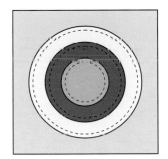

5. Press the blocks. Cut each block into 4 quarters. Each quarter should measure 4½" x 4½".

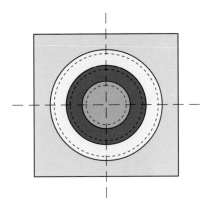

6. Sew 4 different quarter-blocks together to form a Bull's-Eye block.

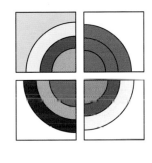

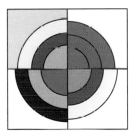

ASSEMBLY AND FINISHING

1. Referring to the photo on page 41, arrange and sew the blocks into 8 rows of 6 blocks each.

2. From the yellow print, cut 6 strips, each 2" x 40". Joining strips as needed to make borders of the correct length, sew the inner border to the top and bottom of the quilt top, then to the sides.

3. From the blue print, cut 7 strips, each 4" x 40". Joining strips as needed to make borders of the correct length, sew the outer border to the top and bottom of the quilt top, then to the sides.

4. Layer the quilt top with batting and backing; baste. Quilt as desired and bind the edges.

5. To fray the circle edges, machine wash your quilt on a gentle cycle, then toss it in the dryer.

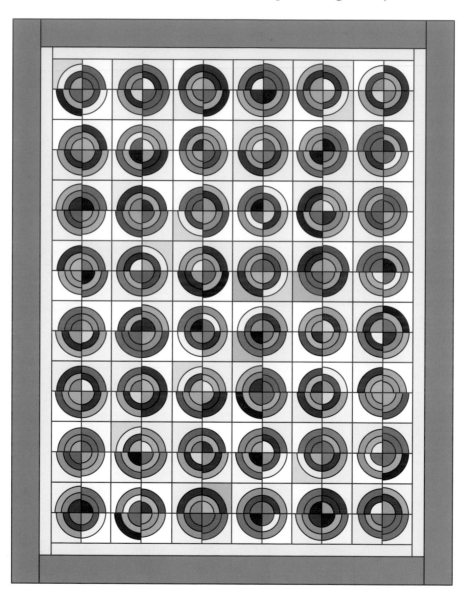

Arabic Lattice

HERE AT COUNTRY Threads, our favorite block is the Log Cabin. Whenever we see an opportunity to divide a block into lights and darks, Log-Cabin–style, we do. The result of our effort is this red-and-black quilt with its Streak of Lightning layout. Although the Arabic Lattice block requires a template for the big triangle, its size makes it fast to sew.

Finished Quilt: 53" x 64"

Finished Block: 11" x 11"

MATERIALS
42"-wide fabric

+ ¼ yd. *total* assorted tan prints for blocks
+ 2 yds. *total* assorted red prints for blocks*
+ 2 yds. *total* assorted black prints for blocks*
+ ⅜ yd. black solid for inner border
+ 3½ yds. for backing
+ ⅜ yd. for binding

   * Pieces need to be at least 6" x 13" for the large triangles, with the 13" length on the straight grain.

ARABIC LATTICE BLOCK

Cut pieces as indicated in the following chart. You will have enough pieces to make 1 block. Make 20 blocks.

Piece	Fabric	No. of Pieces	Dimensions
#1	Tan	2	2½" x 2½"
#2	Red	1	2½" x 2½"
#3	Black print	1	2½" x 2½"
#4	Red	2	Template 2*
#5	Black print	2	Template 2*

* When using the triangle template, be sure to place the arrow on the straight grain of the fabric.

Sew the first triangle as shown below, stopping 1½" from the corner (this is a partial seam). Add the remaining triangles in the order shown, then finish the partial seam.

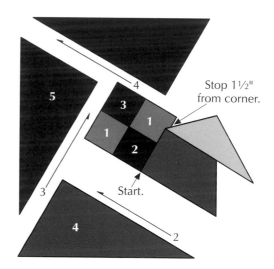

ASSEMBLY AND FINISHING

1. Arrange and sew blocks together in 5 rows of 4 blocks each. Rotate the blocks to create the Streak of Lightning effect, or create your own design.

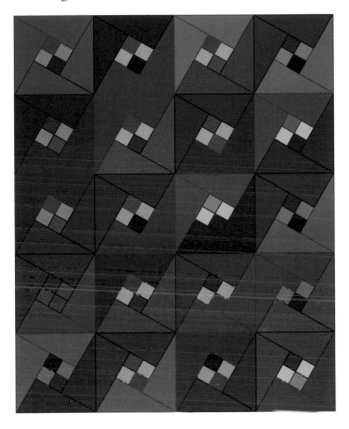

2. From the black solid, cut 6 strips, each 1½" x 40". Joining strips as needed to make borders of the correct length, sew the inner border to the top and bottom of the quilt top, then to the sides.

3. The outer border is called a "chunk" border and is made up of 4"-wide squares and rectangles. From the assorted red and black prints, cut a variety of strips, each 4" wide. Crosscut the strips into random lengths, then join the pieces to make the top and bottom borders, each 46½" long, and 2 side borders, each 64½" long.

4. Sew the top and bottom borders to the quilt top, then add the side borders.

5. Layer the quilt top with batting and backing; baste. Quilt as desired and bind the edges.

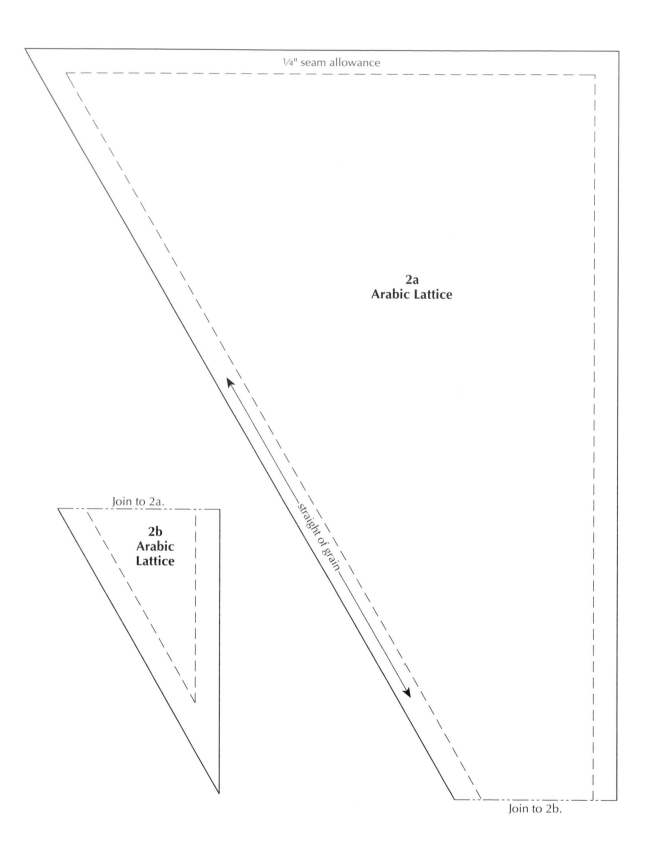

¼" seam allowance

2a
Arabic Lattice

straight of grain

Join to 2a.

2b
Arabic
Lattice

Join to 2b.

Jacob's Ladder I

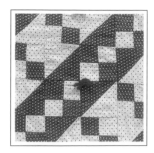

JACOB'S LADDER I relies on controlled bands of color for its design. Turn to page 52 to see an entirely different quilt made with the same block.

Finished Quilt: 30" x 30"
Finished Unit: 3" x 3"

MATERIALS
42"-wide fabric

+ ½ yd. *total* assorted light prints for units
+ ½ yd. *total* assorted dark prints for units
+ ¼ yd. tan stripe for border
+ 1 yd. for backing
+ ¼ yd. for binding

BLOCK UNITS

From the light prints, cut:
+ 64 squares, each 2" x 2"
+ 16 squares, each 3⅞" x 3⅞"; cut each square once diagonally to make 32 half-square triangles

From the dark prints, cut:
+ 64 squares, each 2" x 2"
+ 16 squares, each 3⅞" x 3⅞"; cut each square once diagonally to make 32 half-square triangles

1. Join 2" light and dark squares to make four-patch units.

Make 32.

2. Join light and dark triangles to make half-square triangle units.

Make 32.

ASSEMBLY AND FINISHING

1. Arrange and sew the units together.

2. From the tan stripe, cut 8 rectangles, each 3½" x 12½". From the dark prints, cut 12 squares, each 3½" x 3½". Sew 3½" squares to the right-hand ends of 4 rectangles and to the left-hand ends of 4 other rectangles. Trim the outer edge of each square (page 13).

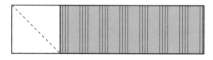

Make 4.

Make 4.

3. Sew the border units together as shown.

Make 2 for top and bottom borders.

Make 2 for side borders.

4. Sew the top and bottom borders to the quilt top, then add the side borders.

5 Layer the quilt top with batting and backing; baste. Quilt as desired and bind the edges.

Jacob's Ladder II

THIS, OUR SECOND JACOB'S Ladder quilt, came out of a "what if" brainstorm session. An evening's work resulted in the small, scrappy quilt—pieced, quilted, and bound by morning.

Finished Quilt: 45" x 62"
Finished Block: 6" x 6"

MATERIALS
42"-wide fabric

+ 2 yds. yellow-and-blue plaid for background
+ ⅛ yd. purple print #1 for four-patch units
+ ⅛ yd. purple print #2 for four-patch units
+ ⅛ yd. purple print #3 for four-patch units
+ ⅛ yd. red print #1 for four-patch units
+ ⅛ yd. red print #2 for four-patch units
+ ¼ yd. red print #3 for half-square triangles
+ ⅛ yd. green print #1 for four-patch units
+ ⅛ yd. green print #2 for four-patch units
+ 1⅜ yds. green print #3 for half-square triangles, outer border, and binding
+ ½ yd. pink plaid for inner border (cut on bias)
+ 3 yds. for backing
+ ⅜ yd. for binding

UNITS

From the yellow-and-blue plaid, cut:
+ 7 strips, each 2" x 40"
+ 7 strips, each 2" x 10"
+ 4 strips, each 3⅞" x 40". Cut the strips into a total of 39 squares, each 3⅞" x 3⅞"; cut each square once diagonally.

From *each* purple fabric, red #1 and #2, and green #1 and #2, cut:
+ 1 strip, 2" x 40" (7 strips total)
+ 1 strip, 2" x 10" (7 strips total)

From red #3, cut:
+ 2 strips, each 3⅞" x 40". Cut the strips into a total of 17 squares, each 3⅞" x 3⅞"; cut each square once diagonally.

From green #3, cut:
+ 3 strips, each 3⅞" x 40". Cut the strips into a total of 22 squares, each 3⅞" x 3⅞"; cut each square once diagonally.

1. Sew each of the 2"-wide purple, red, and green strips to a 2"-wide yellow-and-blue plaid strip to make strip units in two different lengths, 40" and 10". Cut 24 segments, each 2" wide, from each matching set of strip units. Keep the segments separated by color.

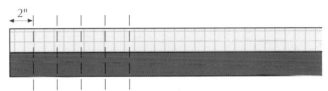

2. Join matching segments to make four-patch units. Make 12 units of each color.

Make 12
of each color.

3. Sew red #3 and green #3 triangles to the yellow-and-blue plaid triangles to make half-square triangle units.

Make 34 red.   Make 44 green.

ASSEMBLY AND FINISHING

1. From the yellow-and-blue plaid, cut 4 squares, each 12" x 12"; cut each square twice diagonally to make 16 side triangles. Cut 2 squares, each 8" x 8"; cut each square once diagonally to make 4 corner triangles.

2. Arrange the four-patch units and triangle units in vertical rows by color. Starting in the upper left corner, sew units together in groups of 4 to make blocks.

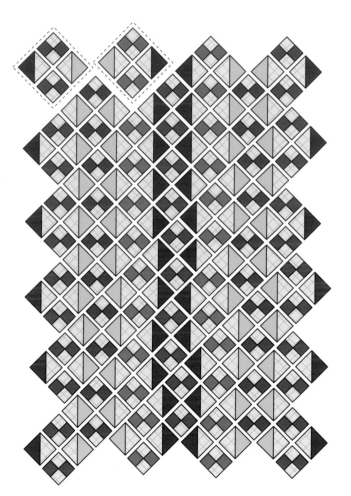

3. Arrange and sew the blocks and side triangles in diagonal rows. Add the corner triangles last. The triangles are oversized and will be trimmed in the next step.

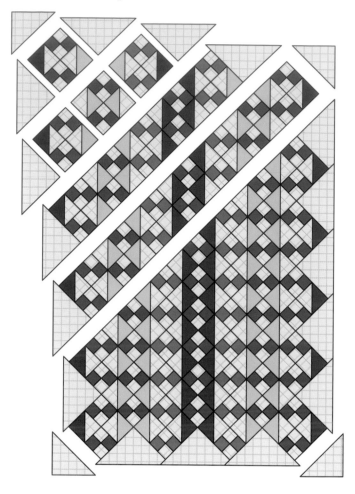

4. Trim the triangles 1½" from the block corners.

5. From the pink plaid, cut enough 1½"-wide bias strips to equal approximately 190" in length. Joining strips as needed to make borders of the correct length, sew the inner border to the top and bottom of the quilt top, then to the sides.

6. From green print #3, cut 5 strips, each 4" x 40". Joining strips as needed to make borders of the correct length, sew the outer border to the top and bottom of the quilt top, then to the sides.

7. Layer the quilt top with batting and backing; baste. Quilt as desired and bind the edges.

Slashed Album

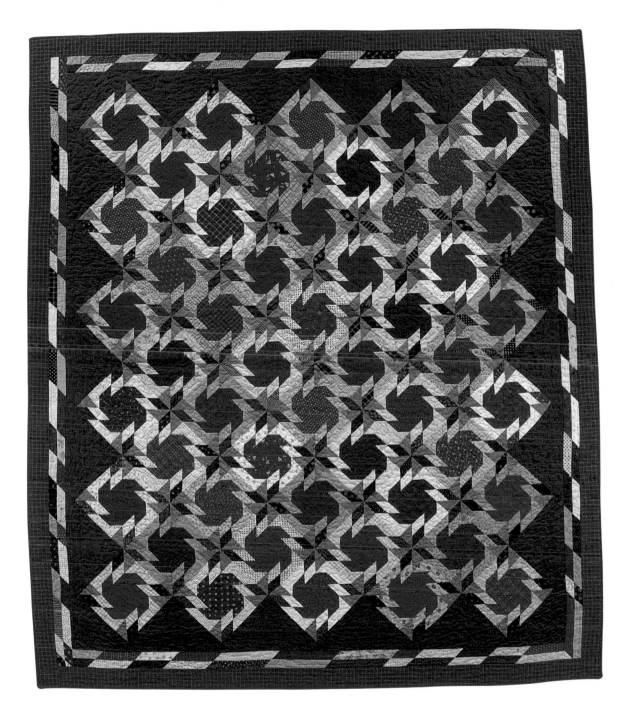

OUR SLASHED ALBUM block doesn't look much like Aunt Amy's, since we altered the design to accommodate Template-Free cutting and quick-piecing techniques. We arranged the colors to form secondary patterns and chose to make the quilt very scrappy. Slashed Album is truly a Country Threads classic—a perfect "firecracker" of a quilt for the Fourth of July.

Finished Quilt: 84" x 98"

Finished Block: 10"

MATERIALS
42"-wide fabric

+ 3½ yds. *total* assorted tan prints for backgrounds
+ 2¾ yds. *total* assorted red prints for block centers and strip piecing
+ 1⅜ yds. *total* assorted blue prints for strip piecing
+ 1 yd. blue-and-white check for half-square triangles in blocks
+ 2 yds. blue-and-black check for side and corner triangles
+ 1⅛ yds. red-and-blue plaid for outer border
+ 8 yds. for backing
+ ½ yd. for binding

SLASHED ALBUM BLOCKS

From the tan prints, cut;
+ 50 strips, each 1¾" x 40"
+ 100 squares, each 3⅜" x 3⅜"; cut each square once diagonally

From the red prints, cut:
+ 25 strips, each 1¾" x 40"
+ 50 squares, each 5½" x 5½" (Cut 2 squares to match each red strip.)

From the blue prints, cut:
+ 25 strips, each 1¾" x 40"

From the blue-and-white check, cut:
+ 10 strips, each 3⅜" x 40". Cut the strips into a total of 100 squares, each 3⅜" x 3⅜"; cut each square once diagonally.

1. Sew a 1¾"-wide red strip to a 1¾"-wide tan strip. Make 25 strip units. From each strip unit, cut 8 segments, each 2¼" wide, at a 45-degree angle. Cut a total of 200 red/tan segments. Reserve the remainder of each strip unit for the inner pieced border.

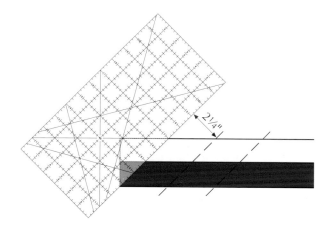

2. Repeat step 1 with blue and tan strips to make 200 blue/tan segments.

3. Sew a red/tan and a blue/tan segment together as shown. Add a blue-and-white check triangle to the right-hand end and a tan triangle to the left-hand end. Using matching red, blue, and tan fabrics, make 4 pieced units for each block.

Make 4 for each block.

4. Sew a section to the right side of a matching red center square. Stitch from the corner of the square to the halfway point (this is a partial seam). Sew 3 matching sections to the remaining sides of the square in the order shown. Finish the partial seam to complete the block.

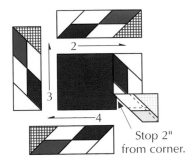

Stop 2" from corner.

ASSEMBLY AND FINISHING

1. From the blue-and-black check, cut 5 squares, each 18" x 18". Cut each square twice diagonally to make side triangles. (You will use only 18.) Cut 2 squares, each 11" x 11". Cut each square in half once diagonally to make corner triangles.

2. Arrange and sew the blocks and side triangles in diagonal rows. Add the corner triangles last. The side and corner triangles are oversized and will be trimmed in the next step.

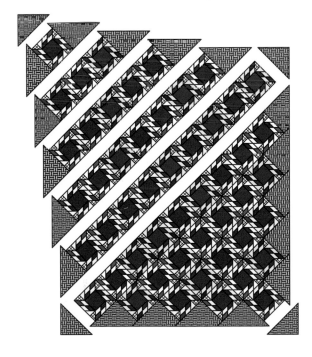

3. Trim the corner and side triangles 1¾" from the block corners.

4. Trim both ends of each leftover strip unit at a 45-degree angle. Cut the segments randomly into smaller units if desired. Alternating red and blue, join the segments end to end to make the top and bottom borders, each approximately 75" long, and 2 side borders, each approximately 94" long. Sew the borders to the quilt.

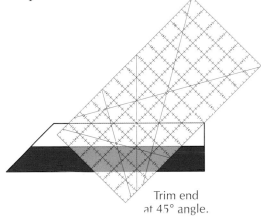

Trim end at 45° angle.

5. From the red/blue/tan plaid, cut 10 strips, each 3¼" x 40". Joining strips as needed to make borders of the correct length, sew the outer border to the top and bottom of the quilt top, then to the sides.

6. Layer the quilt top with batting and backing; baste. Quilt as desired and bind the edges.

Drunkard's Path I

DRUNKARD'S PATH is a traditional block, often made with just two colors. We updated our version with a scrappy look—our block is quite different from Aunt Amy's original. We like making scrap quilts and this one was no exception.

Finished Quilt: 38½" x 52½"

Finished Unit: 3½" x 3½"

MATERIALS

42"-wide fabric

- 1¼ yds. *total* assorted light prints for Drunkard's Path units
- 1⅞ yds. *total* assorted dark prints for Drunkard's Path units
- ½ yd. burgundy print for border
- 1¾ yds. for backing
- ¼ yd. for binding
- Freezer paper

DRUNKARD'S PATH BLOCKS

Cut pieces as indicated in the following chart. Make 30 blocks.

Piece	Fabric	No. of Pieces	Dimensions
#1	Lights	9	8" x 8"
#1	Darks	21	8" x 8"
#2	Lights	21	6" circle
#2	Darks	9	6" circle

Cut 30 circles, each 5½" in diameter, from freezer paper. Center, then press a paper circle onto the wrong side of a 6" fabric circle. Press the ¼" seam allowance over the edge of the freezer paper. Remove the freezer-paper circle and reuse until it no longer sticks to fabric. Appliqué the circles to the squares by hand or machine.

 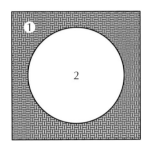

Make 9.   Make 21.

ASSEMBLY AND FINISHING

1. Cut each appliquéd square into quarters.

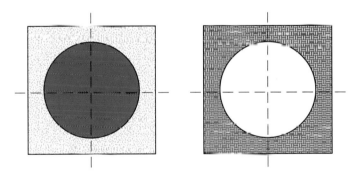

2. From the assorted dark prints, cut 20 squares, each 4" x 4". Referring to the photo on the facing page, arrange and sew together the units and 4" squares.

3. From the burgundy print, cut 5 strips, each 2¼" x 40". Joining strips as needed to make borders of the correct length, sew the border to the top and bottom of the quilt top, then to the sides.

4. Layer the quilt top with batting and backing; baste. Quilt as desired and bind the edges.

Drunkard's Path II

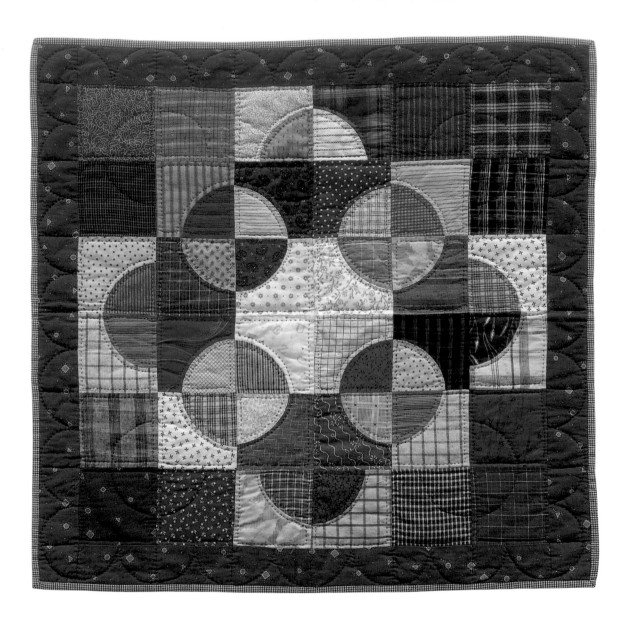

THIS SMALL Drunkard's Path quilt stitches up quickly. Make a scrappy quilt as shown, or pick your favorite contrasting colors to make a traditional two-color design. Make extra blocks and you'll have enough to make several quilts at once.

Finished Quilt: 25" x 25"
Finished Unit: 3½" x 3½"

MATERIALS
42"-wide fabric

- ½ yd. *total* assorted light prints for units
- ½ yd. *total* assorted dark prints for units
- ¼ yd. dark print for border
- ¾ yd. for backing
- ¼ yd. for binding
- Freezer paper

DRUNKARD'S PATH UNITS

Cut pieces as indicted in the following chart. You will have enough pieces to make 6 blocks.

Piece	Fabric	No. of Pieces	Dimensions
#1	Lights	4	8" x 8"
#1	Darks	2	8" x 8"
#2	Lights	2	6" circle
#2	Darks	4	6" circle

Cut 6 circles, 5½" in diameter, from freezer paper. Center, then press a paper circle on the wrong side of a 6" fabric circle. Press the ¼" seam allowance over the edge of the freezer paper. Remove the freezer-paper circle and reuse until it no longer sticks to the fabric. Appliqué circles (piece #2) by hand or machine.

 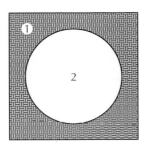

Make 8.   Make 4.

ASSEMBLY AND FINISHING

1. Cut each appliquéd square into quarters.

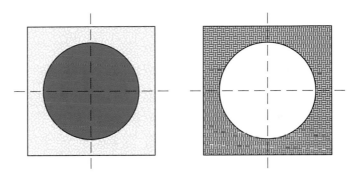

2. From the assorted dark prints, cut 12 squares, each 4" x 4". Arrange and sew together the units and 4" squares.

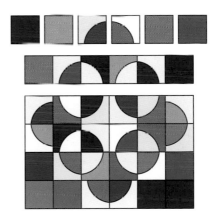

3. From the dark print, cut 2 strips, each 2½" x 21½", for the top and bottom edges, and 2 strips, each 2½" x 25½", for the sides. Sew the border strips to the top and bottom first, then to the sides.

4. Layer the quilt top with batting and backing; baste. Quilt as desired and bind the edges.

Drunkard's Path III

WE WANTED TO make a traditional Drunkard's Path quilt using only two contrasting colors, but since we like scrappy quilts so much, we decided to use a variety of red and brown prints for the darks and a variety of gold prints for the lights.

Finished Quilt: 26" x 50"
Finished Unit: 3½" x 3½"

MATERIALS
42"-wide fabric

+ 1 yd. *total* assorted light gold prints for units
+ ⅝ yd. *total* assorted red and brown prints for units
+ ⅔ yd. *total* assorted red prints for pieced border
+ 1½ yds. for backing
+ ¼ yd. for binding
+ Freezer paper

DRUNKARD'S PATH UNITS

Cut pieces as indicted in the following chart. You will have enough pieces to make 17 blocks.

Piece	Fabric	No. of Pieces	Dimensions
#1	Lights	17	8" x 8"
#2	Darks	17	6" circle

Cut 17 circles, each 5½" in diameter, from freezer paper. Center, then press a paper circle on the wrong side of a 6" fabric circle. Press the ¼" seam allowance over the edge of the freezer paper. Remove the freezer-paper circle and reuse until it no longer sticks to the fabric. Appliqué circles (piece #2) by hand or machine.

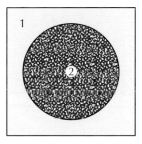

Make 17.

ASSEMBLY AND FINISHING

1. Cut each appliquéd square into quarters.

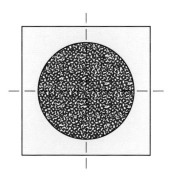

2. From the assorted gold prints, cut 16 squares, each 4" x 4". Arrange and sew together the units and 4" squares.

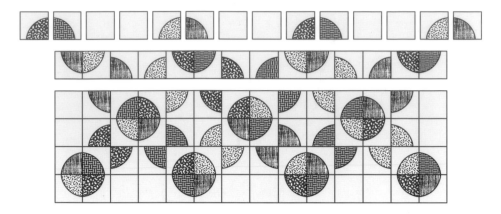

3. From the assorted red prints, cut 20 rectangles, each 4" x 7½", and 4 squares, each 4" x 4".

4. Join 3 rectangles to make each of 2 side borders. Sew the borders to the sides of the quilt. Join 7 rectangles to make each of 2 borders for the top and bottom edges. Add a square to each end of the pieced borders. Sew the borders to the top and bottom edges.

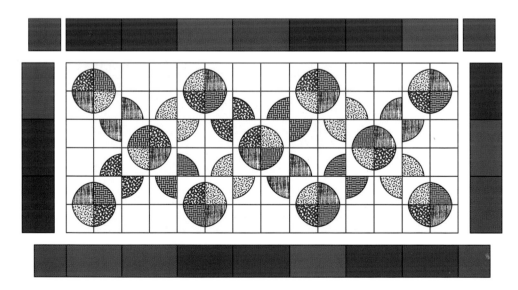

5. Layer the quilt top with batting and backing; baste. Quilt as desired and bind the edges.

Dove in the Window

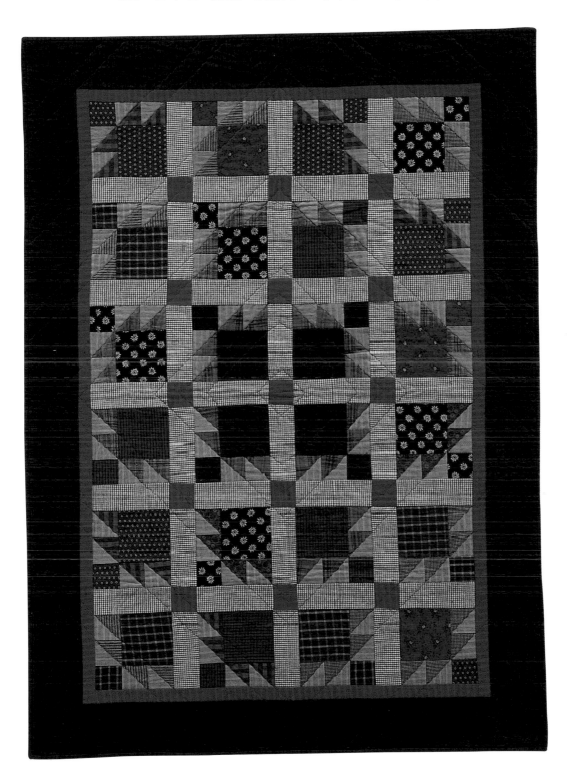

WE LOVE THE COLOR combination of pumpkin orange and federal blue. Once we chose the color scheme, the layout fell into place. We featured one Dove in the Window block in the center of our quilt and surrounded it with quarter units and sashing. You can easily make a larger quilt by adding more quarter units around the center block.

Finished Quilt: 40" x 56"

Finished Unit: 6" x 6"

MATERIALS
42"-wide fabric

◆ ⅝ yd. *total* assorted dark blue prints for blocks
◆ ⅜ yd. *total* assorted medium blue prints for blocks
◆ ⅜ yd. *total* assorted tan prints for blocks
◆ ⅝ yd. blue check for sashing
◆ ⅜ yd. orange stripe for cornerstones and inner border
◆ ¾ yd. blue stripe for outer border
◆ 2½ yds. for backing
◆ ⅜ yd. for binding

DOVE IN THE WINDOW UNIT

Using pieces #1–4, cut and piece 24 units. The cutting directions are for 1 block.

Piece	Fabric	No. of Pieces	Dimensions
#1	Dark blue	1	4½" x 4½"
#2	Dark blue	1	2½" x 2½"
#3	Medium blue	2	2⅞" x 2⅞" ◲
#3	Tan	2	2⅞" x 2⅞" ◲

ASSEMBLY AND FINISHING

1. From the blue check, cut 38 rectangles, each 2½" x 6½".

2. From the orange stripe, cut 15 squares, each 2½" x 2½", for cornerstones.

3. Referring to the illustration on the facing page, arrange and sew the pieced units, sashing strips, and cornerstones together in rows. Notice the orientation of the four center units. The units are rotated to make the traditional Dove in the Window block. The remaining units are positioned around the center block, with the large square facing the center.

4. From the orange stripe, cut 4 strips, each 1½" x 40". Joining strips as needed to make borders of the correct length, sew the inner border to the top and bottom of the quilt top, then to the sides.

5. From the blue stripe, cut 5 strips, each 4½" x 40". Joining strips as needed to make borders of the correct length, sew the outer border to the top and bottom of the quilt top, then to the sides.

6. Layer the quilt top with batting and backing; baste. Quilt as desired and bind the edges.

Wedding Ring I

SINCE THIS Wedding Ring variation makes such an interesting secondary design, we wanted to keep the block small so we could see a larger pattern. It's a block we would never have used without Aunt Amy to inspire us, but the terrific finished quilt made us glad that we did.

Finished Quilt: 26" x 26"
Finished Unit: 5" x 5"

MATERIALS
42"-wide fabric

+ 1 yd. *total* assorted blue prints for blocks and pieced border
+ 1 yd. tan print for block backgrounds and pieced border
+ ⅛ yd. red-orange print for blocks and corner squares
+ ⅜ yd. blue print for border
+ ⅞ yd. for backing
+ ¼ yd. for binding

WEDDING RING BLOCKS

Cut pieces as indicated in the following chart. You will have enough pieces to make 1 block. Make 16 blocks.

Piece	Fabric	No. of Pieces	Dimensions*
#1	Blue	4	1½" x 1½"
#2	Blue	8	1⅞" x 1⅞" ◹
#3	Tan	4	1½" x 1 ½"
#4	Tan	8	1⅞" x 1⅞" ◹
#5	Red-Orange	1	1½" x 1½"

* If you prefer to quick-piece the half-square triangles, do not cut the 1⅞" squares. Instead, cut 1½"wide strips on the bias. Join the strips and cut 1½" squares from the strip unit. You will need 36" of bias strip unit to cut 16 bias squares for each block.

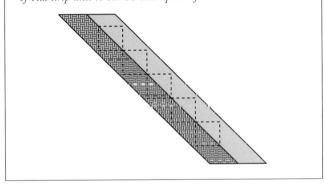

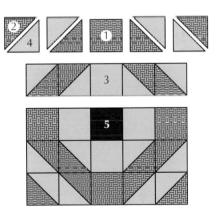

ASSEMBLY AND FINISHING

1. Referring to the illustration at right, arrange and sew the blocks in 4 rows of 4 blocks each.

2. Cut 18 squares, each 1⅞" x 1⅞", from the assorted blue prints, and 18 squares, each 1⅞"x 1⅞", from the tan print. Cut each square once diagonally. Join the blue and tan triangles to make half-square triangle units.

3. From the tan print, cut 16 rectangles, each 1½" x 3½". Join the triangle units and tan rectangles to make the inner borders as shown.

Make 2 for top and bottom borders.

Make 2 for side borders.

4. Sew the borders to the top and bottom of the quilt top. Sew the remaining borders to the sides.

5. From the blue print for the border, cut 4 strips, each 2½" x 22½". Sew the borders to the sides of the quilt top. From the red-orange fabric, cut 4 corner squares, each 2½" x 2½". Sew a square to each end of the remaining border strips and add these to the top and bottom of the quilt top.

6. Layer the quilt top with batting and backing; baste. Quilt as desired and bind the edges. Since there are more than 40 seams in each block, we recommend quilting in-the-ditch.

Wedding Ring II

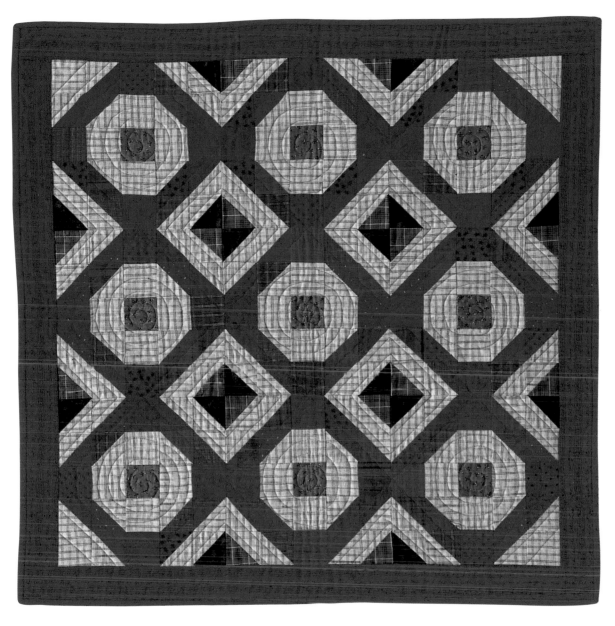

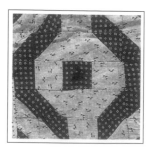

WE TRIED this block in a 10" version just to see if it would be easier to sew together than the 5" block shown on page 68—and it was. We used an assortment of red fabrics for the rings, and teal for the squares and outer triangles. The contemporary look is one of controlled scraps.

Finished Quilt: 33½" x 33½"
Finished Unit: 10" x 10"

MATERIALS
42"-wide fabric

- ⅝ yd. *total* assorted red prints for blocks
- ⅞ yd. tan print for blocks
- ¼ yd. *total* assorted teal prints for blocks
- ⅜ yd. red print for border
- ¼ yd. for binding

WEDDING RING BLOCKS

Cut pieces as indicated in the following chart. You will have enough pieces to make 1 block. Make 5 blocks.

Piece	Fabric	No. of Pieces	Dimensions*
#1	Red	4	2½" x 2½"
#2	Red	6	2⅞" x 2⅞" ◻
#3	Tan	4	2½" x 2½"
#4	Tan	8	2⅞" x 2⅞" ◻
#5	Teal	1	2½" x 2½"
#6	Teal	2	2⅞" x 2⅞" ◻

* If you prefer to quick-piece the half-square triangles, do not cut the 2⅞" squares. Instead, cut 2¼" wide strips on the bias. Join the strips and cut 2½" squares from the strip unit. Cut 16 bias squares for each block.

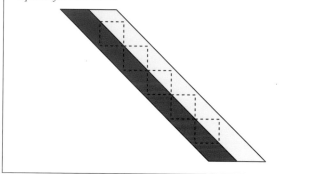

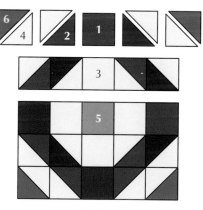

Block A

Cut pieces as indicated in the following chart. You will have enough pieces to make 1 block. Make 4 blocks.

Piece	Fabric	No. of Pieces	Dimensions
#1	Red	4	2½" x 2½"
#2	Red	6	2⅞" x 2⅞" ◳
#3	Tan	5	2½" x 2½"
#4	Tan	8	2⅞" x 2⅞" ◳ *
#5	Teal	1	2½" x 2½"
#6	Teal	2	2⅞" x 2⅞" ◳ **

* *You'll use only 15 triangles in the block.*

** *You'll use only 3 triangles in the block.*

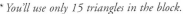

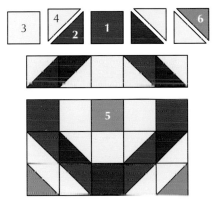

Block B

ASSEMBLY AND FINISHING

1. Arrange and sew the blocks in 3 rows of 3 blocks each, placing a Block B in each corner. Rotate Block B so that the tan square is at the outer corner.

Tan square

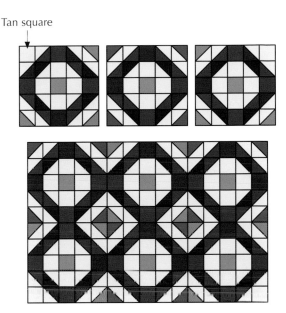

2. From the red print, cut 2 strips, each 2¼" x 30½", for the top and bottom edges, and 2 strips, each 2¼" x 34", for the sides. Sew the border strips to the top and bottom first, then to the sides.

3. Layer the quilt top with batting and backing; baste. Quilt as desired and bind the edges.

Shooting Star

A BIT OF whimsy prompted this medallion-style quilt in which 8" Shooting Star blocks corral goats, chickens, cows, and sheep. We simplified Aunt Amy's block, changing diamonds to half-square triangle units, and we fused the animals for fast appliqué.

We want to make a whole quilt of just chicken blocks—all with different personalities. Chickens rule at Country Threads.

Finished Quilt: 54" x 54"
Finished Pinwheel Blocks: 8" x 8"
Finished Animal Blocks: 11½" x 11½"

MATERIALS
42"-wide fabric

- ¾ yd. *total* assorted tan prints for Shooting Star blocks
- ¾ yd. *total* assorted brown prints for Shooting Star blocks
- ⅔ yd. total assorted red prints for Shooting Star blocks
- 4 squares, each 12" x 12", assorted tan prints for animal blocks
- ¾ yd. *total* assorted prints for animal blocks
- ⅛ yd. dark print #1 for sashing
- ⅛ yd. dark print #2 for first border
- ⅜ yd. *total* assorted scraps for second (pieced) border
- ⅛ yd. red print for third border
- ¼ yd. dark print #3 for fourth border
- ¾ yd. dark print #4 for fifth border
- 3½ yds. for backing
- ⅜ yd. for binding
- 5 small buttons for eyes
- Paper-backed fusible web

ANIMAL BLOCKS

Cut and piece 4 animal blocks. Fuse the appliqué pieces in numerical order to the 12" background squares, leaving a ¼"-wide seam allowance at the edge of the block (except when placing the body). For the animal bodies, position the fabric on the background square and trim any excess even with the square.

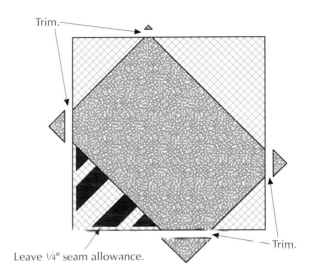

Trim.

Trim.

Leave ¼" seam allowance.

If desired, buttonhole-stitch the raw edges of the appliqués. You can stitch by hand, or you can use your sewing machine if it makes a buttonhole stitch. Add buttons for eyes and embroider legs on the chicken.

COW

Use the templates on page 82.

Piece	Fabric	No. of Pieces	Dimensions
#1–4	Legs	1 each	Templates 1–4
#5	Tail	1	Template 5
#6	Body	1	8¾" x 10⅛"
#7	Ear	1	Template 7
#8	Ear	1	Template 8
#9	Head	1	3¼" x 7"
#10	Nose	1	1¼" x 3¼"
#11	Star	1	Star template

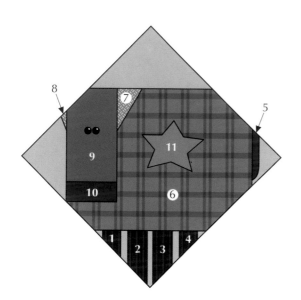

GOAT

Use the templates on page 80.

Piece	Fabric	No. of Pieces	Dimensions
#1–4	Legs	1 each	Templates 1–4
#5	Beard	1	Template 5
#6	Horn	1	Template 6
#7	Head	1	2⅛" x 3½"
#8	Body	1	6¾" x 11¼"
#9	Star	1	Star template

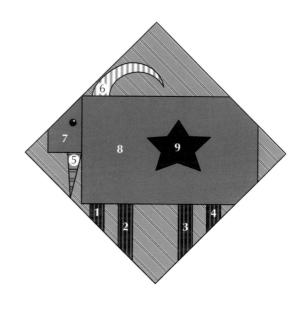

SHEEP

Use the templates on page 81.

Piece	Fabric	No. of Pieces	Dimensions
#1–4	Legs	1 each	Templates 1–4
#5	Tail	1	Template 5
#6	Face	1	Template 6
#7	Body	1	8" x 11¼"
#8	Ear	1	Template 8
#9	Star	1	Star template

CHICKEN

Use the templates on page 83.

Piece	Fabric	No. of Pieces	Dimensions
#1	Wattle	1	Template 1
#2	Beak	1	Template 2
#3	Comb	2	Template 3
#4	Body	1	8¾" x 10⅝"
#5	Wing	1	Template 5
#6	Star	1	Star template

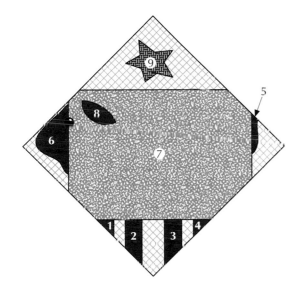

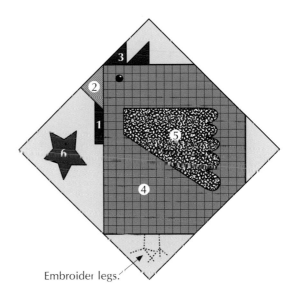

Embroider legs.

PINWHEEL BLOCKS

Cut pieces as indicated in the following chart. You will have enough pieces to make 1 block. Make 20 blocks.

Piece	Fabric	No. of Pieces	Dimensions
#1	Tan	4	2½" x 2½"
#2	Tan	4	2⅞" x 2⅞"
#3	Red	8	2⅞" x 2⅞"
#4	Brown	4	2½" x 2½"
#5	Brown	4	2⅞" x 2⅞"

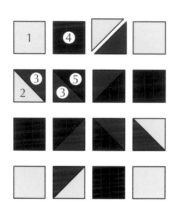

ASSEMBLY AND FINISHING

1. From dark print #1, cut 4 strips, each 1" x 12", for sashing strips. Cut 1 red square, 1" x 1".

2. Sew together the blocks, sashing strips, and square.

3. From dark print #2, cut 4 border strips, each 1" x 40". Sew the borders to the top and bottom of the quilt top, then to the sides.

4. From the assorted scraps for the second border, cut 60 squares, each 2¼" x 2¼". Join 14 squares to make each of 2 borders. Sew the borders to opposite sides of the quilt top. Join 16 squares to make each of 2 borders. Sew the borders to the remaining sides of the quilt top.

5. From the red print, cut 4 border strips, each 1" x 40". Sew the borders to opposite sides of the quilt top, then to the remaining sides.

6. From dark print #3, cut 4 border strips, each 2" x 40". Sew the borders to opposite sides of the quilt top, then to the remaining sides.

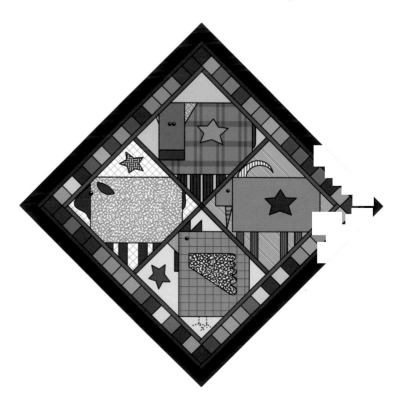

7. Sew the Shooting Star blocks to the center section.

8. From dark print #4, cut 6 border strips, each 3½" x 40". Joining strips as needed to make borders of the correct length, sew the borders to opposite sides of the quilt top, then to the remaining sides.

9. Layer the quilt top with batting and backing; baste. Quilt as desired and bind the edges.

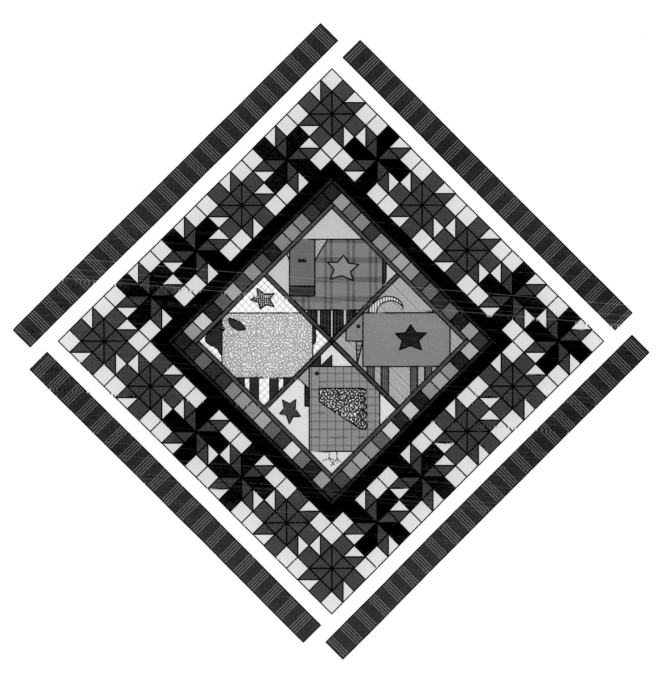

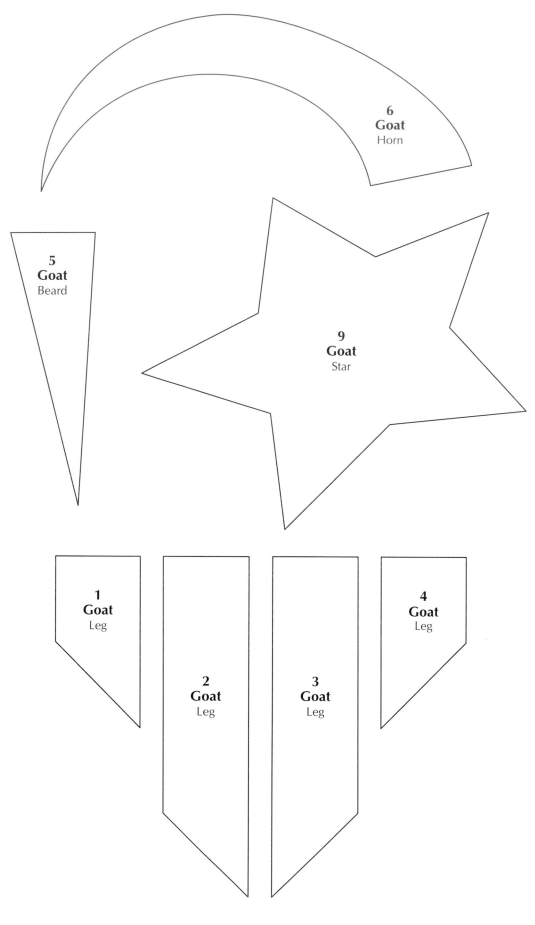

6
Goat
Horn

5
Goat
Beard

9
Goat
Star

1
Goat
Leg

2
Goat
Leg

3
Goat
Leg

4
Goat
Leg

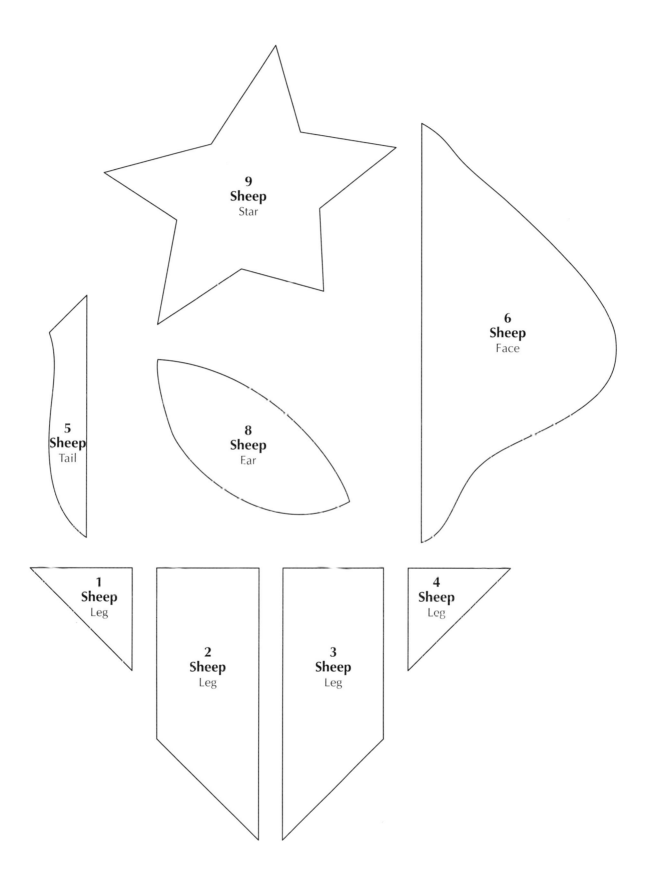

9
Sheep
Star

6
Sheep
Face

5
Sheep
Tail

8
Sheep
Ear

1
Sheep
Leg

4
Sheep
Leg

2
Sheep
Leg

3
Sheep
Leg

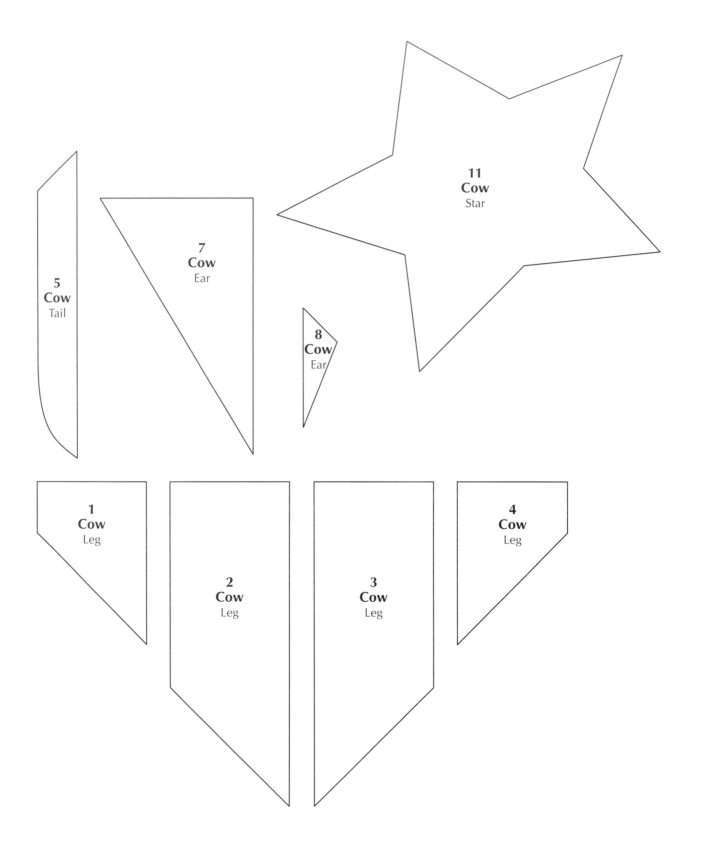

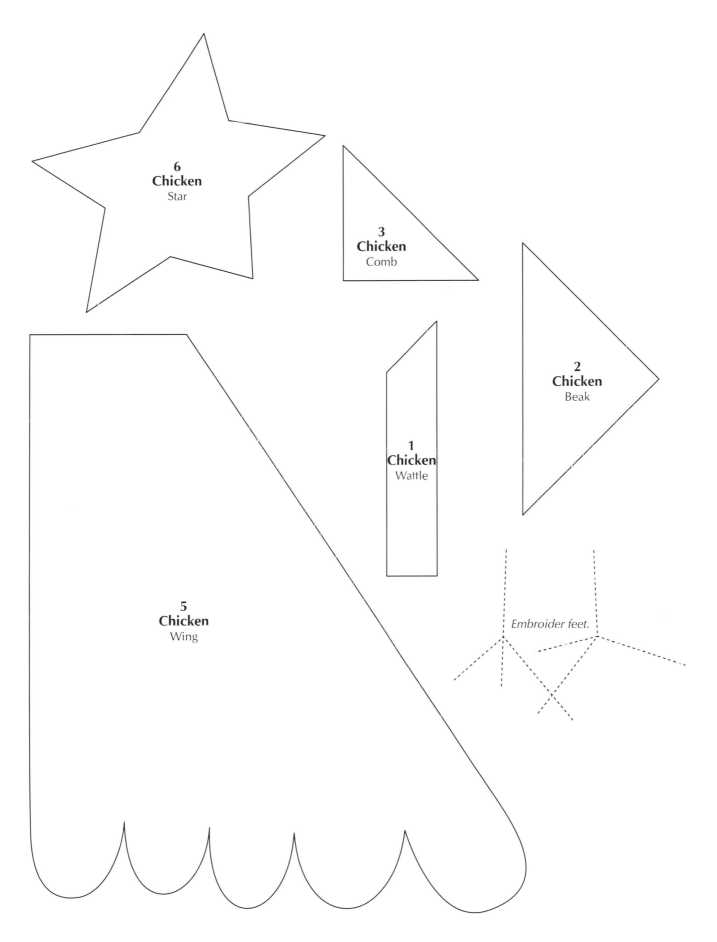

6
Chicken
Star

3
Chicken
Comb

2
Chicken
Beak

1
Chicken
Wattle

5
Chicken
Wing

Embroider feet.

MAKE A SMALLER quilt featuring just one of the animals. We've featured the chicken in our quilt, but you can use any of the animal blocks on pages 76–77 for this quilt.

Finished Quilt: 22 x 31¾"
Finished Animal Blocks: 11½" x 11½"

MATERIALS
42"-wide fabric

- ⅜ yd. *total* assorted prints for animal block
- 1 tan print square, 12" x 12", for animal block
- 2 green stripe squares, each 12½" x 12½", for background triangles
- ⅛ yd. orange-and-green check for inner border
- ⅛ yd. *total* assorted prints for pieced border
- ¼ yd. tan-and-green check for outer border
- ⅔ yd. for backing
- ¼ yd. for binding
- 1 small button for eye
- Paper-backed fusible web

ANIMAL BLOCK

Referring to "Animal Blocks" on pages 75–77, cut and piece 1 chicken or other animal block of your choice. Fuse the appliqué pieces in numerical order to the 12" tan print square, leaving a ¼"-wide seam allowance at the edges of the block, except where the body butts up to the edge. After positioning the animal body on the background square, trim any excess even with the edge of the square. Use a buttonhole stitch on the raw edges of the appliqué shapes if desired. You can do this by hand, or by machine if your machine has this capability. Add buttons for eyes, and embroider legs if you're using the chicken.

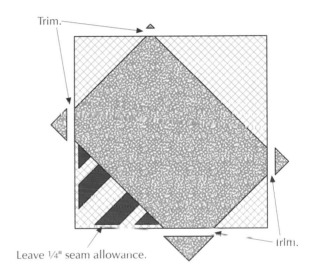

Trim.

Leave ¼" seam allowance.

Trim.

CHICKEN

Piece	Fabric	No. of Pieces	Dimensions
#1	Wattle	1	Template 1
#2	Beak	1	Template 2
#3	Comb	2	Template 3
#4	Body	1	8¾" x 10⅝"
#5	Wing	1	Template 5
#6	Star	1	Star template B

ASSEMBLY AND FINISHING

1. Cut both 12½" green stripe squares in half once diagonally to yield 4 half-square triangles. Sew 2 triangles to opposite sides of the chicken block. Trim the corners of the triangle even with the sides of the block.

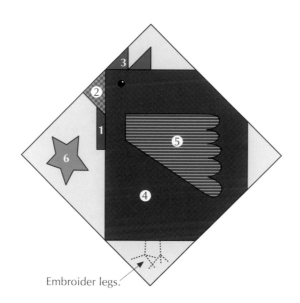

Embroider legs.

2. Sew a triangle to each remaining side. Trim the background triangles 2" from the top and bottom of the block, and 1⅛" from the sides. The block should measure 18½" x 20¼" (including seam allowances) after trimming.

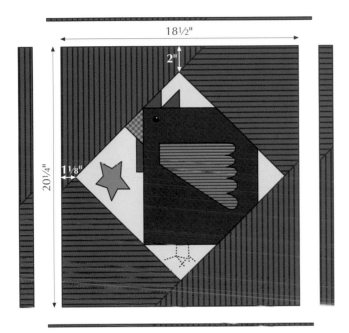

3. From the orange and green stripe, cut 2 strips, each 2½" x 18½". Sew the strips to the top and bottom edges.

4. From the assorted prints, cut 18 squares, each 2½" x 2½". Join 9 squares to make each of 2 pieced borders.

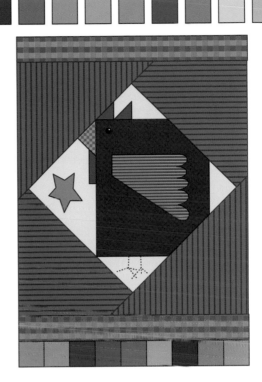

5. Sew the pieced borders to the top and bottom edges.

6. From the tan and green check, cut 2 strips, each 2½" x 18½", for the top and bottom edges, and 2 strips, each 2½" x 32¼", for the sides. Sew the border strips to the top and bottom first, then to the sides.

7. Layer the quilt top with batting and backing; baste. Quilt as desired and bind the edges.

Quiltmaking Basics

ROTARY CUTTING

Instructions for quick-and-easy rotary cutting are provided wherever possible. All measurements include standard ¼-wide seam allowances. For those unfamiliar with rotary cutting, a brief introduction follows.

1. Fold the fabric and match selvages, aligning the crosswise and lengthwise grains as much as possible. Place the folded edges closest to you on the cutting mat. Align a square ruler along the folded edge of the fabric. Then place a long, straight ruler to the left of the square ruler, just covering the uneven raw edges of the left side of the fabric.

    Remove the square ruler and cut along the right edge of the long ruler, rolling the rotary cutter away from you. Discard this strip. (Reverse this procedure if you are left-handed.)

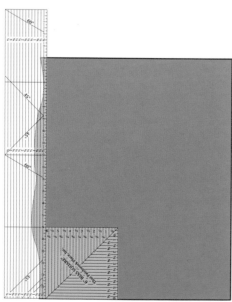

2. To cut strips, align the required measurement on the ruler with the newly cut edge of the fabric. For example, to cut a 3"-wide strip, place the 3" ruler marking at the edge of the fabric.

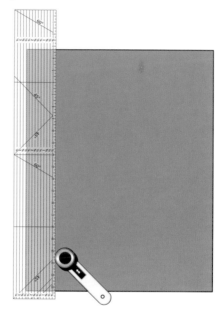

3. To cut squares, cut strips in the required widths. Trim away the selvage ends of the strip. Align the required measurement on the ruler with the left edge of the strip and cut a square. Continue cutting squares until you have the number needed.

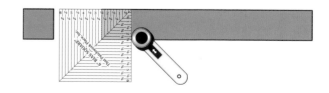

MACHINE PIECING

Making Templates

Most blocks are designed for easy rotary cutting and quick piecing. Some blocks, however, require templates. Templates for machine piecing include ¼" seam allowances. Use plastic or cardboard to make the templates. Mark the pattern name and grain-line arrow on the template, and mark seam intersections on the fabric to make joining pieces easier.

Seam Allowances

The most important thing to remember when machine piecing is to maintain a consistent ¼"-wide seam allowance. Otherwise, the quilt block will not be the desired finished size. If that happens, the size of everything else in the quilt is affected, including alternate blocks, sashings, and borders. Measurements for all components are based on blocks that finish accurately to the desired size plus ¼" on each edge for seam allowances.

Take the time to establish an exact ¼"-wide seam guide on your machine. Some machines have a special quilting foot that measures exactly ¼" from the center needle position to the edge of the foot. This feature allows you to use the edge of the presser foot to guide the fabric for a perfect ¼"-wide seam allowance.

If your machine doesn't have such a foot, create a seam guide by placing the edge of a piece of tape or moleskin, or a magnetic seam guide, ¼" away from the needle.

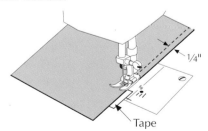

Chain Piecing

Chain piecing is an efficient system that saves time and thread.

1. Sew the first pair of pieces from cut edge to cut edge, using 12 to 15 stitches per inch. At the end of the seam, stop sewing but do not cut the thread.

2. Feed the next pair of pieces under the presser foot, as close as possible to the first pair. Continue feeding pieces through the machine without cutting the thread in between. There is no need to backstitch, since each seam will be crossed by another seam.

3. When all pieces have been sewn, remove the chain from the machine and clip the threads between the pieces.

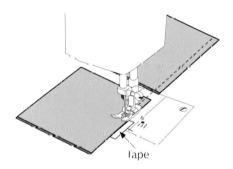

Easing

If two pieces being sewn together are slightly different in size (less than ⅛"), pin the place where the two pieces should match, and in the middle if necessary, to distribute the excess fabric evenly. Place the longer piece on the bottom when you stitch the seam. The feed dogs will ease the two pieces together.

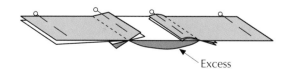

Pressing

The traditional rule in quiltmaking is to press seams to one side, toward the darker color wherever possible. Press the seam flat from the wrong side first, then press the seam in the desired direction from the right side. Press carefully to avoid distorting the shapes.

When joining two seamed units, plan ahead and press the seam allowances in opposite directions. This reduces bulk and makes it easier to match seam lines. Where two seams meet, the seam allowances will butt against each other, making it easier for you to join units with perfectly matched seam intersections.

Opposing seams

FUSIBLE APPLIQUÉ

1. Trace or draw your shape on the paper side of fusible web. Cut out the shape, leaving a generous margin all around the outline.

NOTE: If the appliqué pattern is directional, you need to make a reverse tracing so the pattern will match the original when it is pressed in place. Otherwise, you'll get a reversed image. You don't need to make reverse tracings for patterns that are symmetrical.

2. Fuse the shape to the wrong side of your fabric.

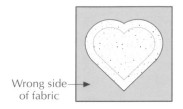

Wrong side of fabric

3. Cut out the shape exactly on the line.

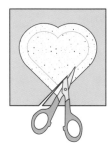

4. Remove the paper, position the shape on the background, and press in place.

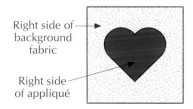

Right side of background fabric

Right side of appliqué

5. If desired, secure the edges with a blanket stitch or running stitch.

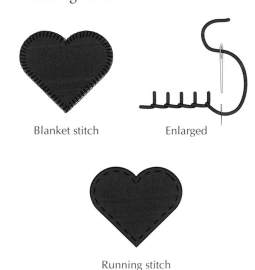

Blanket stitch   Enlarged

Running stitch

QUILT TOP ASSEMBLY

Squaring Up Blocks

When your blocks are complete, take the time to square them up. Use a large square ruler to measure your blocks and make sure they are the desired size plus an extra ¼" on each edge for seam allowances. For example, if you are making 6" blocks, they should all measure 6½" before you sew them together. Trim the larger blocks to match the size of the smallest one. Be sure to trim all four sides; otherwise your block will be lopsided.

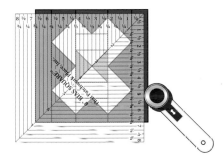

If your blocks are not the required finished size, you will have to adjust all the other components of the quilt accordingly.

Making Straight-Set Quilts

1. Arrange the blocks as directed in the quiltmaking instructions.

2. Sew blocks together in horizontal rows; press the seams in opposite directions from row to row.

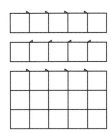

Straight-Set Quilts

3. Sew the rows together, making sure to match the seams between the blocks.

Making Diagonally Set Quilts

1. Arrange the blocks, side triangles, and corner triangles as directed in the quiltmaking instructions.

2. Sew the blocks together in diagonal rows; press the seams in opposite directions from row to row.

3. Sew the rows together, making sure to match the seams between the blocks. Sew the corner triangles on last.

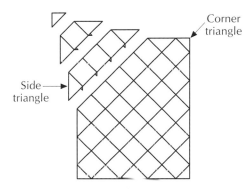

Diagonally Set Quilts

Adding Borders

For best results, do not cut border strips and sew them directly to the quilt sides without measuring first. The edges of a quilt often measure slightly longer than the distance through the quilt center, due to stretching during construction. To get accurate results, measure the quilt top through the center in both directions to determine how long to cut the border strips. This step ensures that the finished quilt will be as straight and as "square" as possible.

Plain border strips are commonly cut along the crosswise grain and seamed where extra length is needed. Borders cut from the lengthwise grain of fabric require extra yardage, but seaming the required length is then unnecessary.

Straight-Cut Borders

1. Measure the width of the quilt top through the center. Cut border strips to that measurement, piecing as necessary. Mark the center of the quilt edges and the border strips. Pin the borders to the top and bottom of the quilt top, matching the center marks and ends and easing as necessary. Sew the border strips in place. Press the seams toward the borders.

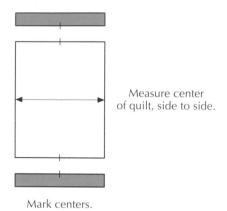

Measure center
of quilt, side to side.

Mark centers.

2. Measure the length of the quilt top through the center, including the top and bottom borders just added. Cut border strips to that measurement, piecing as necessary; mark the center of the quilt edges and the border strips. Pin the borders to the sides of the quilt top, matching the center marks and ends and easing as necessary; stitch. Press the seams toward the borders.

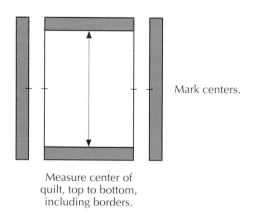

Mark centers.

Measure center of
quilt, top to bottom,
including borders.

Borders with Corner Squares

1. Measure the width and length of the quilt top through the center. Cut border strips to those measurements, piecing as necessary. Mark the center of the quilt edges and the border strips. Pin the side borders to opposite sides of the quilt top, matching centers and ends and easing as necessary. Add the side border strips; press the seams toward the border.

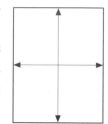

2. Cut corner squares of the required size (the cut width of the border strips). Sew one corner square to each end of the remaining two border strips; press seams toward the border strips. Pin the border strips to the top and bottom edges of the quilt top. Match centers, seams between the border strip and corner square, and ends, easing as necessary; stitch. Press seams toward the border.

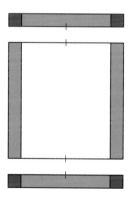

QUILTING

Marking the Quilting Lines

Whether or not to mark the quilting designs depends upon the type of quilting you will be doing. Marking is not necessary if you plan to quilt in-the-ditch or outline quilt a uniform distance from seam lines. For more complex quilting designs, mark the quilt top before the quilt is layered with batting and backing.

Choose a marking tool that will be visible on your fabric and test it on scraps to be sure the marks can be removed easily. Masking tape can also be used to mark straight quilting. Tape only small sections at a time and remove the tape when you stop at the end of the day; otherwise, the sticky residue may be difficult to remove from the fabric.

Layering the Quilt

The quilt "sandwich" consists of backing, batting, and the quilt top. Cut the quilt backing at least 4" larger than the quilt top all the way around. For large quilts, it is usually necessary to sew two or three lengths of fabric together to make a backing of the required size. Trim away the selvages before piecing the lengths together. Press the backing seams open to make quilting easier.

 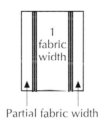

Two lengths of fabric seamed in the center   Partial fabric width

Batting comes packaged in standard bed sizes, or it can be purchased by the yard. For large quilts, piece two lengths or two widths of backing fabric together. Use low-loft cotton batting for large quilts. Use low-loft, dense fleece for wall hangings.

1. Spread the backing, wrong side up, on a flat, clean surface. Anchor with pins or masking tape. Be careful not to stretch the backing out of shape.

2. Spread the batting over the backing, smoothing out any wrinkles.

3. Place the pressed quilt top on the batting. Smooth out any wrinkles and make sure the edges of the quilt top are parallel to the edges of the backing.

4. Starting in the center, baste with needle and thread and work diagonally to each corner. Continue basting in a grid of horizontal and vertical lines 6" to 8" apart. Finish basting around the edges.

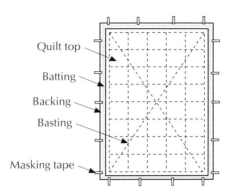

Quilt top
Batting
Backing
Basting
Masking tape

NOTE: For machine quilting, you may baste the layers with #2 rust-proof safety pins. Place pins about 6" to 8" apart, away from the area you intend to quilt.

Hand Quilting

To quilt by hand, you will need short, sturdy needles (called "Betweens"), quilting thread, and a thimble to fit the middle finger of your sewing hand. Most quilters also use a frame or hoop to support their work. Use the smallest needle you can comfortably handle; the finer the needle, the smaller your stitches will be.

1. Thread your needle with a single strand of quilting thread about 18" long; make a small knot and insert the needle in the top layer about 1" from the place where you want to start stitching. Pull the needle out at the point where quilting will begin and gently pull the thread until the knot pops through the fabric and into the batting.

2. Take small, evenly spaced stitches through all 3 quilt layers.

3. Rock the needle up and down through all layers, until you have 3 or 4 stitches on the needle. Place your other hand underneath the quilt so you can feel the needle point with the tip of your finger when a stitch is taken.

4. To end a line quilting, make a small knot close to the last stitch; then backstitch, running the thread a needle's length through the batting. Gently pull the thread until the knot pops into the batting; clip the thread at the quilt's surface.

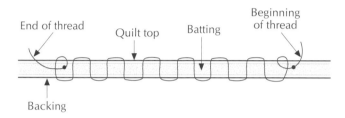

End of thread   Quilt top   Batting   Beginning of thread

Backing

Machine Quilting

Machine quilting is suitable for all types of quilts, from crib to full-size bed quilts. With machine quilting, you can quickly complete quilts that might otherwise languish in closets. Marking is necessary only if you need to follow a grid or a complex pattern. It is not necessary if you plan to quilt in-the-ditch, outline quilt a uniform distance from seam lines, or free-motion quilt in a random pattern.

For straight-line quilting, it is extremely helpful to have a walking foot to help feed the quilt layers through the machine without shifting or puckering. Some machines have a built-in walking foot; other machines require a separate attachment.

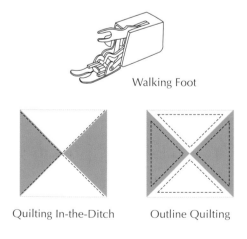

Walking Foot

Quilting In-the-Ditch   Outline Quilting

For free-motion quilting, you need a darning foot and the ability to drop the feed dogs on the machine. With free-motion quilting, you do not turn the fabric under the needle but instead guide the fabric in the direction of the design. Use free-motion quilting to outline quilt a pattern or to create stippling or other curved designs.

Darning Foot

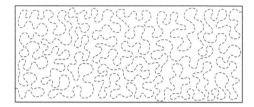

Free-Motion Quilting

FINISHING

Binding

To make straight-grain binding strips, cut 1½"-wide strips across the width of the fabric. You will need enough strips to go around the perimeter of the quilt plus 10" for seams and the corners in a mitered fold.

To attach binding:

1. Join strips at right angles and stitch across the corner as shown to make 1 long piece of binding. Trim excess fabric and press seams open.

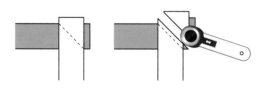

Joining Straight-Cut Strips

2. Trim the batting and backing even with the quilt top.

3. Starting on one side of the quilt and using a ¼"-wide seam allowance, stitch the binding to the quilt, keeping raw edges even with the quilt-top edge. End the stitching ¼" from the corner of the quilt and backstitch. Clip the thread.

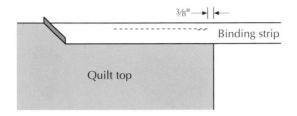

4. Turn the quilt so that you will be stitching down the next side. Fold the binding up, away from the quilt.

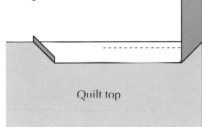

5. Fold the binding back down onto itself, parallel with the edge of the quilt. Begin stitching ⅜" from the edge, backstitching to secure.

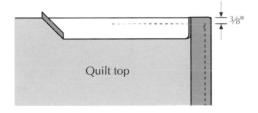

6. Repeat on the remaining edges and corners of the quilt. When you reach the beginning of the binding, overlap the beginning stitches by about 1" and trim any excess binding.

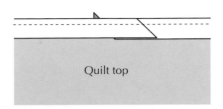

7. Turn the edge of the binding under ¼" and fold it to the back of the quilt, covering the row of machine stitching. Blindstitch in place. A miter will form at each corner. Blindstitch the mitered corners in place.

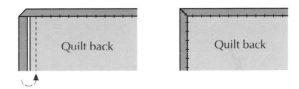

SIGNING YOUR QUILT

Be sure to sign and date your quilt. Future generations will be interested to know more than just who made it and when. Labels can be as elaborate or as simple as you desire. The information can be handwritten, typed, or embroidered. Be sure to include the name of the quilt, your name, your city and state, the date, the name of the recipient if it is a gift, and any other interesting or important information about the quilt.

✌ About the Authors ✌

Mary Tendall Etherington and **Connie Tesene** met in 1981 and soon discovered a shared love of folk art, quilts, antiques, and animals. Their friendship led to a business partnership, the Country Threads quilt shop, which they operate on Mary's farm near Garner, Iowa.

Quilts from Aunt Amy follows Mary and Connie's best-selling That Patchwork Place book, *Life in the Country with Country Threads.*